THE HUMAN
MANIFESTO

A GENERAL PLAN FOR HUMAN SURVIVAL

THE HUMAN MANIFESTO

A GENERAL PLAN FOR HUMAN SURVIVAL

VINCENT L. SCARSELLA

MILL CITY PRESS
MINNEAPOLIS, MN

Mill City Press, Inc.
212 3rd Avenue North, Suite 290
Minneapolis, MN 55401
612.455.2294
www.millcitypublishing.com

ISBN - 978-1-934937-80-8
ISBN - 1-934937-80-0
LCCN - 2009903387

Cover Design and typeset by Kristeen Wegner

Printed in the United States of America

The idea of death, the fear of it, haunts the human animal like nothing else; it is a mainspring of human activity - designed largely to avoid the fatality of death, to overcome it by denying in some way that it is the final destiny of man....

It seems that the experiment of man may well prove to be an evolutionary dead end, an impossible animal – one who, individually, needs for healthy action the very conduct that, on a general level, is destructive to him.

Who knows what form the forward momentum of life will take in the time ahead or what use it will make of our anguished searching. The most that any one of us can seem to do is to fashion something— an object or ourselves—and drop it into the confusion, make an offering of it, so to speak, to the life force.

- Ernest Becker

To my wife, Rosanne,

and our children,

Derek, Kristyn and Vincent,

and, of course,

to their children and their children.

TABLE OF CONTENTS

PREFACE

Is mankind doomed?

In the Pulitzer Prize winning, *The Denial of Death* (1973) and *Escape From Evil* (1975), social anthropologist, Ernest Becker, suggested that extinction may indeed be mankind's ultimate, evolutionary destiny. After spending years studying what motivates human behavior – why human beings do the things they do, especially evil and destructive things - Becker concluded that mankind's advanced intelligence, the evolutionary trait responsible for the species' survival and dominion over the Earth, may ironically become the cause of its demise.

According to Becker, a byproduct of advanced intelligence is awareness by individual members of the human species that they are nothing more than flesh and blood creatures whose sophisticated minds are trapped in physical bodies which inevitably decay and die. In short, awareness of death is the offspring of intelligence and consciousness. The problem for mankind is thus his godlike nature: man is both aware of the wonder of the world, but that he is not long for it. And it is the torment of this knowledge that has driven him to distraction, and to evil.

The consciousness of life and death, and the related idea that because of death, life is a meaningless and futile struggle solely to remain alive by gorging on other living things, and to perpetuate the species by engaging in sexual relations, imposes a severe anxiety, or "terror," on the human psyche, which is termed in this Manifesto, the ***death/meaninglessness anxiety***. Drawing upon Soren Kierkegaard's interpretation of the Fall of Adam and Eve in The Book of Genesis, as it relates to the human condition, Becker explained: "The fall into self-consciousness, the emergence from comfortable ignorance in nature, had one great penalty for man: it gave him *dread*, or anxiety." Or, as renowned psychiatrist and writer, Irvin D. Yalom, put it in <u>Staring At The Sun: Overcoming the Terror of Death</u>: "Self-awareness is a supreme gift, a treasure as precious as life. This is what makes us human. But it comes with a costly price: the wound of mortality. Our existence is forever shadowed by the knowledge that we will grow, blossom, and, inevitably, diminish and die." Thus, as Becker glumly noted, death is the "worm at the core" of human existence.

In response to the anxiety spawned by the consciousness of death, symbolic methods have naturally arisen among human cultures that offer their members with the means of constructing life immortality projects, or *life illusions,* for repressing that anxiety. These illusions hide, obscure or completely overcome the prospect of death by giving meaning to the lives of a culture's members through methods offered by the culture for self-esteem construction that include the promise of personal immortality. The individual is thus able to function in the world, to act as if life mattered, albeit with the specter of death ever-present, haunting one's every thought and deed and lurking in the shadows of the illusion of one's life.

The awareness of death thus becomes buried within one's psyche by the false belief in the meaning of life inspired by the symbolic action system offered by the culture in which one resides. As Becker put it: "…everything that man does in his symbolic world is an attempt to deny and overcome his grotesque fate. He literally drives himself into a blind obliviousness with social games, psychological tricks, personal preoccupations so far removed from the reality of his situation that they are forms of madness – agreed madness, shared madness, disguised and dignified madness, but madness all the same."

These symbolic forms of the cultural "madness" that enable humans to overcome the psychological terror of death, which Becker termed, "hero systems," are derived from beliefs which arise and develop over time in the culture based upon its socio-economic, political and religious history. Cultural hero systems motivate human behavior by inspiring its members to construct illusions and then act upon them in the pursuit of "heroism" – that is, self-esteem, as well as a connection to personal immortality in a supernatural, "beyond," inhabited and dominated by a "God."

Thus, the death/meaninglessness anxiety is overcome or repressed through illusory "life/immortality projects" (henceforth termed in this Manifesto, **Life Immortality Elusions**, or **LIEs**) constructed from a matrix of methods offered by the hero system of culture in which one resides. In sum, one's life is a mere symbolic illusion, or LIE, constructed solely in order to repress the reality of death. And it is one's LIE that directs or motivates his or her behavior. Therefore, cultural hero systems are the motivational forces directing all human behavior.

Based upon these ideas, it is the essential premise of this Manifesto that mankind's historic inability to rise above barbaric or trivial pursuits and reach its potential as a species stem from the failure of its cultural hero systems to foster illusions among its members that motivate actions advancing beneficial individual and collective ends. A corollary principle of this assertion is that these failed hero systems, including those of modern cultures, that have amply demonstrated an inability to motivate positive and constructive human behavior, must be discarded and replaced by systems that do. Lastly, this Manifesto will describe a hero system, based upon basic beliefs in the sanctity of human life and existence of God, that can motivate positive and constructive human behavior and provide a way for mankind to reach its highest potential. This system is termed in these pages: **The Genuine Hero System.**

The hero systems which have arisen among cultures throughout history have failed to enable humans to genuinely overcome the death/meaninglessness anxiety, and/or do so in ways, such as through warfare, or trivial activities, that have little practical or real value for enhancing the quality of human life, for ensuring the survivability of the species, or for gaining a comprehension of the true nature of God and the Cosmos. Indeed, many of the life illusions spawned by past and present cultural hero systems have been, and are, inimical to human advancement and survival. While there is no way of avoiding the human need to construct illusions of some kind to repress the stark reality of death, the trick is in constructing an ideal illusion that benefits both the personal soul and the collective good.

A cursory review of the historical record and the news of today provide ample support for the basic proposition of this book that humanity's past and present cultural hero systems have failed the species, and, worse, lend credence to Becker's grave prognosis that humanity is likely destined for extinction. Indeed, for almost our entire existence as a species, and certainly over the past 6,000 years of recorded history, human conduct has been marked by violence, cruelty, war, ignorance, selfishness, materialism, and a lack of optimal progress in spiritual and intellectual understanding, and in technological achievement and progress.

The cruelty demonstrated in the course of human events certainly corroborates the idea that mankind is one nasty little species destined for extinction. For countless, unbroken years down the centuries of mankind's existence, human beings have killed and maimed each other in numbingly countless way, often engaging in terrible, cruel acts of mayhem and murder, sometimes with unbridled glee.

The twentieth century is particularly illustrative and damning in this regard. Millions have been murdered by their fellow man in an almost unbroken parade of senseless wars in furtherance of national, religious and economic ideologies. That legacy, unfortunately, has carried forth into the present century, and the promise of future peace appears to be the pure whimsy of starry-eyed pacifists and idealistic dreamers without a basic plan to effectuate their utopian vistas. What real hope can there be for a species that spends immense sums of money and intellectual energy and resources producing weapons of mass destruction while millions upon millions upon millions of human beings suffer daily in abject poverty, starvation, ignorance and despair?

No wonder Becker reached the bleak conclusion that mankind's remarkable intelligence, the very evolutionary trait which has helped the species survive and flourish for the past 50,000 to 100,000 years in establishing wide dominion over nature, and to even leap, however slightly, into outer space, may lead the species to its eventual demise by nuclear holocaust, global warming, the unleash of plague, or some other manmade creation of ultimate and ultra-violent disaster.

But even if we are "lucky" enough to avoid mass self-destruction, we remain destined for extinction by the hand of Nature at some indeterminable time, either in the next moment, or a billion years hence. And because the cultural hero systems which have been devised to deny death, and which motivate human behavior, have prevented humanity from achieving its intellectual, spiritual and technological potential, mankind appears forever incapable of obtaining the means of delivering itself from destruction by inevitable natural forces including, but not limited to, reversal of the poles, asteroid or comet impact, stellar explosion, or some other and innumerable possible natural disasters which are likely to occur either in the near or far future.

Despite the species' dismal track record, and the failure of past idealistic formulae, dreams and ideologies for advancing the human spirit and intellect, this Manifesto has the audacity to proclaim that Becker's doomsday forecast may not be inevitable. Humanity need not become an evolutionary dead-end; rather, our intelligence, and the resultant consciousness of reality, may instead serve as mankind's means to peace, plenty, spiritual and intellectual progress and perhaps, immortality.

Thus, instead of the curse it has been for these past eons, the evolutionary trait of superior intelligence may yet become Nature's shining achievement, the pinnacle of natural selection, enabling a species of animate matter, arisen from the dust of the earth, evolved from a protein soup and one-celled life, to conquer death, and to become, itself, a kind of demi-god. In short, contrary to Becker's concerns, the attribute of intelligence may yet become a blessing for humanity, ultimately enabling the species to overcome the anxiety of death and consequent meaninglessness, and also to attain its full spiritual, intellectual and technological potential. Indeed, without such intelligence and awareness, like all species which have come before it, such as the dinosaurs, mankind would meet with certain evolutionary doom. Instead, there is at last the prospect of animate immortality.

Offering what will be termed, *The Genuine Hero System*, this Manifesto not only points out the basic psychological problem that ails human-kind, but also dares to prescribe the means by which human intelligence may be applied toward attaining the highest level of human spiritual, intellectual and technological achievement. This Manifesto lastly presupposes that human intelligence has not only provided the species with the ability to imagine the concept of God, but also has imbued it with the capacity of progressing incrementally to an absolute comprehension of God.

This Manifesto is ultimately about offering a new way for humans to obtain a kind of ideal heroism required to overcome the fear of death – that is, it offers nothing less than a new way of life, a new illusion – "the grandest illusion," if you will, that may direct mankind to its highest potential and thwart the alarm of Becker and others that humanity is a doomed species.

Certainly, attaining the lofty goals set by this Manifesto will require nothing less than a colossal upheaval of human spiritual and intellectual thought, striving, organization, and action, a revolution of almost unimaginable and impossible magnitude. To pull it off, the existing cultural hero systems by which we human beings have constructed our illusions of reality and organized everyday life, and which presently motivates our behavior and everyday actions, must be rejected and discarded. Concomitantly, we must join in accepting The Genuine Hero System, and its action methods offered for attaining personal heroism, as the motivating force in the pursuit of true meaning and purpose in our lives in order to overcome the psychological debilitation of the death/meaninglessness anxiety.

Thus, an initial and central aim of this Manifesto is to debunk historic and modern cultural hero systems, and explain how, because of their deficiency and inability to genuinely resolve the problem of the death/meaninglessness anxiety, they have caused or contributed to destructive and violent human conduct, or have left their adherents empty, unhappy and spiritually and intellectually bankrupt and lost.

Conversely, this Manifesto seeks to inform and convince humans that the Genuine Hero System is based upon a set of beliefs which foster authentic individual meaning and self-esteem, a kind of "true illusion." Equally important, the "religious" component of the Genuine Hero System seeks nothing less than a quest for the identity and nature of the true God Concept.

Essentially stated, the beliefs underlying The Genuine Hero System are based upon love of the human species, love of the human individual, and love for the "God" which "created" the Cosmos. The Genuine Hero System will thus generate individual self-worth directly from action and achievement which enhances the quality of human life both individually and collectively, as well as ensuring the *eternal* survival of the species.

Equally important, the Genuine Hero System instills religious or cosmic meaning in the lives of its adherents by inspiring and compelling them to acknowledge first and foremost the existence of some sort of "beyond," or God Concept, after compelling in them a recognition that at mankind's current spiritual and intellectual development, a comprehension of the God Concept is woefully deficient. Once that acknowledgement is achieved, mankind must be inspired to embark upon a spiritual and intellectual quest, through scientific, intellectual and spiritual examination and discovery, to achieve a complete and full comprehension of God and the Cosmos.

Stated another way, the "religious" component of the Genuine Hero System first involves a simple acceptance of the idea and presence of God as en entity in the Cosmos, with a corollary recognition that, under our current state of intellectual and spiritual knowledge, we are incapable of grasping more than a glimmer of an understanding of God and the Cosmos. The end of such "genuine religion" is to achieve a comprehension of God through further and continuous intellectual and spiritual study and experimentation. The more knowledge we obtain, the closer we get to God, and so on and so on, toward the eventual goal of a complete comprehension of God and the Cosmos, at which point human beings themselves might achieve a sort of Godhood – but now we are certainly getting far ahead of ourselves!

Lastly, this Manifesto provides a blueprint, through a series of gradual, though determined steps, for accomplishing a complete transformation from ineffectual cultural hero systems that have failed mankind for thousands of years to achieve all the species can achieve by applying a Genuine Hero System as the central human motivational force.

This writer is of course mindful of the supreme difficulty, if not near impossibility, of accomplishing what this Manifesto proposes. It seeks nothing less than to change the minds, to re-program, if you will, billions of human minds. Except for those persons disabled by mental illness, through the process of socialization, each of us has acquired a strong faith in, and adherence to, the false beliefs underlying the hero systems offered by the cultures in which we reside from which we have constructed our life immortality elusions motivating us to action in an effort to deny death, albeit in incorrect or destructive ways, and that fail utterly to provide fulfillment. Every human being needs to recognize, first of all, the falsity of our belief systems in order to reject them; and, second, to seek and gain faith in the motivating beliefs underlying the Genuine Hero System. To get to that point, simply put, will be a monumental undertaking.

In conclusion, this Manifesto calls for radical, revolutionary change, a new way of thinking, a new way of life. Every human being will be required to radically alter the manner in which they construct their life immortality projects or LIEs. However, as a first step down the long and winding and difficult path to the utopian vision of human society proposed by this Manifesto, the reader is implored to recognize and agree that unless we start the journey, humanity, as Becker worried, is truly doomed.

I fully acknowledge that what this Manifesto proposes will not be readily understood, accepted, and, certainly, implemented. It calls for a new style of living, an overthrow of the powers that presently control human action. The powerful forces which benefit and profit from the present system will not allow it to be cast aside without strong and perhaps violent opposition. However, the rest of us must remember that what is ultimately at stake is human happiness, fulfillment, and most importantly, survival, not only for this generation, but for eternal human generations to come.

Let us, therefore, begin down the path toward salvation.

Part One

The Failure of Historic and Modern Hero Systems

Man is literally split in two: he has an awareness of his own splendid uniqueness in that he sticks out in nature with a towering majesty, and yet he goes back into the ground a few feet in order blindly and dumbly to rot and disappear forever. It is a terrifying dilemma to be in and have to live with.

Culture is in its most intimate intent a heroic denial of creatureliness.
- Ernest Becker

It was precisely because of these dangers with which nature threatens us that we came together and created civilization, which is also, among other things, intended to make our communal life possible. For the principal tasks of civilization, its raison d'être, is to defend us against nature.
- Sigmund Freud

CHAPTER ONE
AN INDICTMENT OF HUMANITY

*And God saw that the wickedness of man was great in the earth,
and that every imagination of the thoughts of his heart was only
evil continually.*
- Genesis 6:5

History is a nightmare from which I am trying to awaken.
- James Joyce, *Ulysses*

This Manifesto begins with a blunt and unflattering apprais-
al of humanity's conduct and achievements (or dismal lack
thereof) since its rise, through evolution, as the dominant
species on planet earth. The culmination of this examination is an imaginary accusatory instrument, or indictment,
if you will, filed in a fictitious "Court of Life," alleging the
damning charge that the species has squandered the evolutionary gift of superior intelligence by failing to even remotely achieve its spiritual, intellectual and technological
potential. Indeed, humanity is like some misfit, dawdling

and mischievous child, disappointing the lofty expectations and promise of its evolutionary birthright.

Approximately one-hundred thousand years since it arrival on the evolutionary stage as a definitive human species, and after over six thousand years of civilization, humanity should have accomplished much more in all realms of endeavor. Instead, the species has for the most part wasted time and opportunities, and thus still faces the ever-present prospect of global doom either by some natural cataclysm, or by its own hand.

Anthropologists agree that our species, *homo sapiens sapiens* – a.k.a. mankind, evolved to its present physical and mental condition around 50,000 to 100,000 years ago. In addition to its upright posture and ability to walk on two legs, the most notable attribute of the species, of course, is its superior intelligence in comparison with the rest of the animal kingdom. Moreover, the evolution of the brain as the center of such vast intelligence is of a high order never before produced by Nature on this planet.

Thus, humans are easily distinguishable from other animals, and all life, by their ability to think, to reason, to rationalize, and significantly, by their awareness of existence and their place in the environment in which they live. Humans also have developed complex methods of communication and cooperation among themselves. Mankind is the only species to have gained awareness of the reality of its existence and death, and thus developed the need to construct a symbolic answer to the problem of death through cultural means.

Yet, as has been stated, and will be discussed throughout this Manifesto, the superior intellect of the human species is both a benefit and curse. For while intelligence and consciousness have provided humanity with the means of surviving individually and collectively among and above other animal species in a hostile physical environment, it has also cursed mankind with the awareness of its creatureliness, and of the stark reality that individual life ends. In short, while a superiorly evolved brain has enabled the species to survive and dominate the earth, it has also caused the individual to become aware of his or her own death imposing a profound psychological dilemma and dread.

As will be more fully explored later in this Manifesto, the awareness of death, and the anxiety created in the human mind which such awareness spawns, goes a long way in explaining, and perhaps mitigating, mankind's historic and modern behavioral problems and shortcomings, and inability to reach its ultimate potential.

At this juncture, however, it is necessary to clearly and pointedly expose those shortcomings, if for no other reason than to embarrass this Manifesto's readers into facing up to them. And in doing so, it is hoped that the reader will open up to the prospect of revolutionary change in the way human beings are motivated to action and acknowledge that such change is of paramount necessity in order to obtain a better life for all of us, not to mention the achieving the prospect of eternal survival of the species.

The purpose of this indictment then, is to put humanity on the path toward acceptance of the prescription for freedom, survival and hope which this Manifesto audaciously proposes.

(B). The Indictment

The following presents the general charges that could be set forth in an indictment against the human species in some mythical Court of Life.

The action might be styled:
Life vs. Humanity (a.k.a., homo sapiens sapiens)

Charge One:

Failure To Ensure the Quality of Life for All Human Beings

From its evolutionary manifestation between 50,000 to 100,000 years ago, until the present date, Humanity has failed to devise, develop and implement an organizational system, culture, or government, which ensures that all human beings are given a fair, equal and complete opportunity to pursue life, liberty and happiness.

This failure has led to many obvious ills – abject poverty, hunger, the unnecessary spread of violence, disease, ignorance and injustice.

Charge Two:

Failure to Avoid and Prevent Wasteful Conflict and Warfare

From its evolutionary manifestation between 50,000 to 100,000 years ago until the present date, Humanity has failed to devise, develop and implement an organizational system, culture, or government, which prevents groups of individuals from engaging in acts of conflict and supreme violence, otherwise known as warfare, against other groups of individuals.

This failure has resulted in the wasteful and unnecessary

deaths of millions upon million of human beings and in the destruction of entire civilizations and their infrastructure; moreover, in both the waging of, and preparation for, warfare and defense against warfare, the species has wasted incalculable and vast economic, intellectual and scientific resources.

Charge Three

Failure to Properly Seek the Comprehension of God and Nature

From its evolutionary manifestation between 50,000 to 100,000 years ago until the present date, Humanity has failed to devise, develop and implement an organizational system, culture, or government, enabling it to suitably engage in the spiritual, intellectual and scientific study, examination and research so as to develop, over time, a more complete, if not complete, understanding and comprehension of the nature of God and the Cosmos.

This failure has resulted in the acceptance of puerile and false mythical constructs for the explanation of the existence of God and God's relationship with mankind leading to artificial expectations and hopes regarding spiritual justice and personal immortality.

Charge Four

Failure to Ensure the Survivability of the Human Species

From its evolutionary manifestation between 50,000 and

100,000 years ago until the present date, Humanity has failed to devise, develop and implement an organizational system, culture, or government, capable of ensuring the survival of the human species from possible natural or manmade cataclysm, such that it is certain, at the present level of technological achievement of the species, that mankind is doomed to extinction.

This failure puts the species at constant risk of extinction, either by its own doing, or due to some natural cataclysm, such as impact by a comet or asteroid or inevitable death of the sun.

In sum, the human species is chargeable with failing to develop organizational and governmental systems among its cultural groups which provide the maximum quality of life for all members of the species; has failed to avoid destructive behavior among individuals and groups of individuals; has failed to become unified and join in an effort to insure the survival of the species; and, has failed to use its collective intelligence to steadfastly pursue a comprehension of God and the Cosmos.

Surely, the human species must plead guilty to these charges. Simple observation reveals that many millions of human beings wallow in abject poverty, ignorance, and have become ready targets for physical and mental disease and epidemics; wars rage around us in all their cruel stupidity in many parts of the world; and, intellectual and economic resources are wasted in the pursuit of war (aka military defense), materialistic wealth, and other banal pursuits, while so little of such resources are spent in search of the larger questions of the human condition that nag at the very core of our existence.

As a result of these "crimes," against which there can be no defense, the human species has failed to realize its highest potential, spiritually, intellectually, and technologically. In short, we have failed to reach for the stars, and are no closer to eternal survival than we were when we stepped out of the caves of our origins.

However, by entering a collective plea of guilty to these charges, based upon our genuine remorse for missing the opportunity to reach our true potential for so many thousands of years, we can begin the process of rehabilitation and transformation that is necessary if we are ever to achieve greatness as a species and to survive into the next evolutionary cycle.

CHAPTER TWO
CULTURAL HERO SYSTEMS
AS MOTIVATING FORCES

*The fact is that this is what society is and has always been:
a symbolic action system, a structure of statuses and roles,
customs and rules for behavior, designed to serve as a vehicle
for earthly heroism. Each script has a somewhat different
hero system.*
- Ernest Becker

*Society begins to appear much less unreasonable
when one realizes its true function. It is there to help
everyone to keep their minds off reality.*
- Celia Green

*A belief is a lever that, once pulled, moves almost
everything else in a person's life…Your beliefs define
your vision of the world; they dictate your behavior;
they determine your emotional responses to other human beings.*
- Sam Harris

(A). <u>Darwin: Survival of the Fittest</u>

Central to Darwin's theory of evolution is the concept that all forms of life are pre-disposed for self-preservation. Simply put, living things are biologically programmed to keep on living, and each species evolves in a way, through the process of natural selection, to help its members succeed in the survival game.

Physically, at least, we humans are pathetically equipped for succeeding in that game. We possess no exceptional physical trait useful for survival. We lack speed, heightened senses, strength, or any other physical attribute that marks us above other animals in the evolutionary quest that enables certain species over others to rise to the top of the ecological food chain. Humans lack sufficient physical attributes to enable them to readily outrun or outfight natural predators. Indeed, taking quick stock, it must be readily acknowledged that human beings possess no one *physical* characteristic that would explain the species' domination of the planet.

Yet, there can be no argument that the species, *homo sapiens sapiens*, has been extremely successful in the survival game. Indeed, the species has come to dominate the planet, much like the dinosaurs millions of years ago, until an asteroid or some other natural disaster facilitated their extinction.

How is it, then, with our lack of any extraordinary physical trait, that mankind has risen to the top of the heap of earthly species, to become the star celebrity of the animal kingdom, indeed of the kingdom of life, at least on this planet, the present winner of the game of evolutionary domination? The explanation, of course, is the trait of superior intelligence. Simply put, humanity won the evolutionary game simply because it became collectively able to out-think its adversaries, predators and prey, in the animal kingdom.

Natural selection worked to increase the brain capacity and function of the humanoid, bipedal ancestor species of humanity. Quite simply, increased intelligence advanced the survival of human-like groups. As postulated by Becker and other social anthropologists, superior intelligence enabled humans to develop enhanced social skills, becoming a gregarious species where individuals learned to cooperate with each other in groups for the betterment of each other, and the group as a whole.

By the time primates had evolved into the Cro-Magnon man, the direct precursors of the modern humans, about 100,000 years ago, intelligence had advanced to such a degree that humans had gained a distinct advantage over nature, and other animals, including predators, greatly enhancing the human species' prospects for survival. In short, the trait of intelligence led mankind to invent tools and other technological innovations, and to work cooperatively and socially with each other in groups, increasing its ability to survive and eventually to establish advanced civilizations. The end result, as can be seen around us, is that humanity has become the dominate species on the planet.

(B). <u>The Curse of Intelligence: Consciousness and Terror of Death</u>

If consciousness had not been programmed into the human brain, and influenced by the self-preservation instinct, there would be no recognition for the need to avoid dangers, to cooperate with other humans for sustenance and security, and to do those things which optimally advance individual survival and group procreation and proliferation. However, in the process of becoming more intelligent and aware, humans also became conscious not only of the dangers of their surroundings and the fact of the existence of themselves and others, but also of their creatureliness and eventual death, and the concomitant apparent meaninglessness of life.

Thus, with the gift of superior intelligence enabling the species to thrive and dominate over nature, came the curse of self-awareness. We humans have become aware that we are flesh and blood creatures; and, of course, that our flesh and blood eventually and naturally decays, that the human body dies and rots, that eventually, we cease to exist as physical beings, as creatures in the natural, present world. That we die, eventually and ultimately, without exception, and that we then go someplace else, or perhaps, nowhere.

Hence, the essential human paradox - in the evolutionary survival game, the great benefit of superior intelligence and its offspring, consciousness, has also become its greatest curse. And that is the essence of the human condition that ails us all from birth to death. It is the original sin of Adam – awareness of death.

From the dawn of history, human consciousness compelled a search for the meaning of life. In his book, *Civilization: A New History of the Western World*, Roger Osborne put it this way:

> ...humans have always had an impulse to represent the world around them in pictures and images that is, so far as we know, unique. It is a fair assumption that his is connected to, and presumably a by-product of, consciousness. The ability to conceptualize and plan and think ahead gave humans distinct advantages in tool-making, organizing food collection and hunting, and building shelters – all of which offered them a vastly greater potential range of habitation and diet than their primate cousins. But the same consciousness, as we know from

our own experience, has led humans to look for and require meaning from the world around them. The ability to make a spear that will enable a clawless ape to kill a reindeer is part of the same mental equipment that asks whether, for example, the phases of the moon are connected to the weather or to good hunting or to sickness. While most animals deal with the vagaries of the world in a pragmatic, perceptual way, human consciousness rebels against meaninglessness. And so humans have constructed symbols, invented stories and engaged in rituals that bring meaning.

Thus, the evolutionary enhancement of human intelligence in the process of natural selection, which exponentially increased the species' prospects for survival, had the perhaps unintended consequence of providing each member of the human species with the awareness of their own individual death and consequent meaninglessness of life itself.

Becker and others have postulated that this awareness of death is psychologically terrifying, and must be suppressed at all costs in order for the individual to function in the everyday world. Indeed, according to Becker, "that of all things that move man, one of the principal ones is the terror of death."

As the philosopher, Soren Kierkegaard, recognized - life can be both awesome and dreadful. There are moments when we simply relish being alive. Think of walking outside on a beautiful summer morning and feeling the warm comfortable breezes, and looking up into a stark blue sky with a cup of coffee in hand and the morning newspaper under an arm. In that momentary, often fleeting rush, we experience the joy of simply being alive (Paul of Tarsus put the feeling this way: "Rejoice!"); and, then, we sit in our favorite patio chair on that warm summer morning, and read about an awful accident on the expressway the night before that took a young life, and being alive has suddenly been transformed into a dreadful, frightening experience, beset with senseless problems and unpredictable risk. The terror of death seeps into our life in that moment, enlarges and for a time, consumes us, until we turn to the sports pages and lose ourselves within a method of heroism that is based on the false belief that the wins and losses of our favorite baseball team somehow matters beyond our mortality and the mortality of others.

Kierkegaard termed the competing experiences of joy and dread the "paradox of finitude in the context of infinitude." Simply put, the human mind is capable of fantastic thoughts and dreams while also starkly aware that it is encased in a flesh and blood machine that inevitably and eventually decays, dies and rots away. As Becker starkly put it in *Escape From Evil,* "...life on this planet is a gory spectacle, a science-fiction nightmare in which digestive tracts fitted with teeth at one end are tearing away at whatever flesh they can reach, and at the other end are piling up the fuming waste excrement as they move along in search of more flesh." Indeed, this was at center to the revulsion and rejection of Darwin's theory of natural selection. According to Becker, Darwin "showed this bone-crushing, blood-drinking drama in all its elementality and necessity: Life cannot go on without the mutual devouring of organisms....each organism raises its head over a field of corpses, smiles into the sun, and declares life good."

This dreadful side of human life, the idea of our creatureliness, and that we have no real control over our lives, that death is a random process that may strike us at any moment, haunts us like nothing else throughout our lives and renders everything we do or accomplish utterly meaningless. We are not really significant because we are merely animated pieces of flesh destined to die and decompose into worm meat and dust. As Becker so amply and poetically put it: "This is the terror: to have emerged from nothing, to have a name, consciousness of self, deep inner feelings, an excruciating inner yearning for life and self-expression – and with all this yet to die."

As aptly summed up by cultural anthropologists, Sheldon Solomon, Jeff Greenberg, and Tom Pyszczynski, in their article, <u>Tales From the Crypt: On the Role of Death in Life</u>:

> *Thus, from an evolutionary perspective, cognitive complexity has clearly served us well. But an unavoidable consequence of this vast intelligence culminating in consciousness is the explicit and unsettling awareness that death is inevitable, compounded by the concurrent realization that one is perpetually vulnerable to permanent obliteration for reasons that can never be adequately anticipated or controlled.*

Citing the work and ideas of psychoanalyst Gregory Zilboorg, Becker submitted that though the fear of death is suppressed by society, "underneath all appearances [the] fear of death is universally present." As Zilboorg himself wrote:

> *For behind the sense of insecurity in the face of danger, behind the sense of discouragement and depression, there always lurks the basic fear of death…No one is free of the fear of death… We may take for granted that the fear of death is always present in our mental functioning.*

Or, as Becker put it, death is "the worm at the core"

of human happiness, lurking behind everything we do, a shadow over our lives, darkening our every joy and pleasure.

(C). <u>The Psychological Impetus to Deny Death Through Cultural Hero Systems</u>

Of course, living with the curse of the self-awareness of one's eventual and inevitable demise presents an enormously profound and difficult psychological burden for the individual. Thus, in order to function in the world, one's psyche must fashion a method for repressing or obscuring that eventuality that renders one's life meaningful.

As Becker recognized in <u>The Denial of Death</u>:

> ...the fear of death must be present behind all our normal functioning, in order for the organism to be armed toward self-preservation. But the fear of death cannot be present constantly in one's mental functioning, else the organism could not function. It therefore must be repressed.

Quoting Zilboorg, Becker went on to state:

> ...more than to put away and to forget that which was put away and the place where we put it. It means also to maintain a constant psychological effort to keep the lid on and inwardly never relax our watchfulness.

Becker thus postulated that the primary function of human cultural evolution has been, and remains, to provide the individual with methods for deliverance from the horrible psychological burden of death. This is accomplished via systems of beliefs that arise in cultures that provide methods for motivating actions and behavior for its members to enable them to overcome the psychological fear of death by imbuing their lives with meaning. Becker termed these cultural systems, "hero systems." As Becker put it in *Escape From Evil,* his follow-up, ironically posthumous companion to *Denial of Death*: "In *The Denial of Death* I argued that man's innate and all-encompassing fear of death drives him to attempt to transcend death through culturally standardized hero systems and symbols."

In summary, it is impossible for a person to psychologically function in everyday life under the weight of the awareness of death. Therefore, the awareness of death must be repressed – that is, denied; and, it is culture which offers the means and methods by which humans hide the stark and overwhelming reality of death through various methods of action based upon beliefs which have arisen in the culture which are collectively known as cultural hero systems.

As Becker noted:

> *The social hero-system into which we are born marks out our paths for our heroism, paths to which we conform, to which we shape ourselves so that we can please others, become what they expect us to be. And instead of working our inner secret we gradually cover it over and forget it, while we become purely external men, playing successfully the standardized hero game into which we happen to fall by accident, by family connection, by reflex patriotism, or by the simple need to eat and the urge to procreate.*

Ernest Becker, <u>The Denial of Death</u>, 82-83

In his article, "Death Grip," in the August 27, 2007 issue of <u>The New Republic</u>, John B. Judis summarized the essence of Becker's theory as follows:

In The Denial of Death, Becker tried to explain how fear of one's own demise lies at the center of human endeavor. "Man's anxiety," Becker wrote, "results from the human paradox that man is an animal who is conscious of his animal limitation." Becker described how human beings defend themselves against this fundamental anxiety by constructing cultures that promise symbolic or literal immortality to those who live up to established standards. Among other things, we practice religions that promise immortality; produce children and works of art that we hope will outlive us; seek to submerge our own individuality in a larger, enduring community of race or nation; and look to heroic leaders not only to fend off death, but to endow us with the courage to defy it. We also react with hostility toward individuals and rival cultures that threaten to undermine the integrity of our own.

Other authors have similarly characterized Becker's theory for human motivation as being the fulfillment of the individual need to repress the terrorizing prospect of death awareness via culturally engineered illusions, or LIEs, as this Manifesto terms them, which provide the individual with self-esteem that motivates individual and collective human behavior. (For the remainder of this Manifesto, in fact, I will refer to these culturally engineered illusions as *elusions*, since they enable the individual to avoid facing the reality of death, and hence, the person's "life immortality elusion," drawn from the means and methods offered by his or her cultural hero system, can be known by the fitting acronym, "**LIE**").

Donald Carveth, in *The Melancholic Existentialism of Ernest Becker,* an article published in <u>Free Associations</u> Vol. 11, Part 3, No. 59 (2004): 422-29, summarized Becker's theory as follows:

Like Pascal, Kierkegaard and others in the existentialist trad-
ition who write of our constant need for diversion from the dis-
mal reality of our condition, Becker argues that our primary
death anxiety necessarily and quite literally drives us to distrac-
tion. Repression, if not imposed by civilization, would be self-
imposed due to our need to deny the body that, in a variety of
ways, especially in its anal functions, is a constant reminder of
the mortality we cannot face. **Society offers a range of possi-**
bilities for heroism in which death is denied and an illusion
of immortality constructed. (Emphasis added).

Sheldon Solomon, Jeff Greenberg, and Tom Pyszczynski, social scientists who have confirmed Becker's hy-
pothesis in tests of their "terror-management" theory, have
described his death denial/motivational force theory in their
article, <u>Tales From the Crypt: On the Role of Death in Life</u>,
as follows:

Cultural worldviews facilitate effective terror management by
providing individuals with a vision of reality that supplies an-
swers to universal cosmological questions such as Who am I?
Where did I come from? What should I do? What will happen
to me when I die? in ways that imbue the universe with mean-
ing, permanence, and stability and give hope of symbolic or
literal immortality.

Thus, culture is in essence a conglomeration of beliefs, shared by its constituents, and imposed upon them by
the process of familial, educational and societal socialization, giving shape and presence to the nature of reality, the
primary and essential purpose of which is to obliterate or
minimize the anxiety engendered by the uniquely human

awareness of death. Through its own distinctive belief system, each human culture and sub-culture (nations, tribes, families, gangs, etc.) provides its constituents with often firm and unwavering answers to the universal questions regarding the nature of life and meaning and the methods for overcoming the anxiety or fear of death.

Through the mechanism of cultural hero systems, humans gain the means and mechanisms for developing a sense of self-esteem, and an individualized connection to supernatural immortality, or God, and thus drive from their minds the ever-present lurking shadow of mortality. The problem, of course, is that such mechanisms enable the individual to create mere illusions to avoid the reality of death. With the true nature of the human condition hidden, the individual and the group fail to commit to action which most benefits getting to the heart of that condition, and drives individuals to action which is inimical and adverse to human progress and survival, and which is contrary to the pursuit of genuine happiness. And even more problematic for the individual is the sense somewhere within the soul, the "worm at the core," that tells them that the life he or she is leading is illusory lacking in true and eternal meaning beyond the physical realm. Is it any wonder that so many people are unhappy, going about their daily grind, at Thoreau put it, "in quiet desperation."

(D). Constructing the LIE from Cultural Hero Systems

In *The Denial of Death* (1973) and *Escape from Evil* (1975), Ernest Becker hypothesized that humans are compelled by their awareness of death and creatureliness to construct illusions giving meaning to their lives using symbolic belief systems offered by the cultures in which they reside. Such belief systems provide methods for denying the reality of death and motivate and direct human behavior. The illusions, which we have termed LIEs, thus hide or repress the anxiety which the stark prospect of death, and the fact that we are gorging, shitting creatures, engenders within the psyches of each of us.

In general, then, as Becker put it: "Culture is in its most intimate intent, a heroic denial of creatureliness," and therefore, death. Thus, as Becker fittingly noted, "heroism is first and foremost a reflex of the terror of death." Indeed, it is the premise of *The Denial of Death* that death is the "mainspring" of all human action. Each cultural hero system must therefore satisfy the human need for individual special-ness, while also providing the promise of an existence after one's death – that is, something beyond the physical or creaturely realm.

Mankind resolves the problem of death by using the same cognitive and psychological capabilities that engendered the problem of death anxiety/meaninglessness in the first place. The formidable mental power of humanity resulting in the awareness of death and meaninglessness of life in the face of that stark fact is put to use through the development in cultures of symbolic action systems, based upon various beliefs which have arisen and been accepted as true by that culture. These cultural action systems enable its members to repress - or as Becker put it - deny death, by enabling them to construct illusory projects – individual life immorality illusions – to do so. As Becker further stated: "...everything that man does in his symbolic world is an attempt to deny and overcome his grotesque fate. He literally drives himself into a blind obliviousness with social games."

Citing the Austrian psychologist and one time Freudian, Otto Rank, Becker postulated that the psychological mechanism of "transference" or "projection" explains how the individual forms an attachment to, or identification with, the force or concept, whether it be animate or inanimate, a live object or an ideal, to give meaning to one's existence. The person latches onto another person as a romantic love interest, or out of sexual lust, or blindly follows the charismatic leader, or celebrity; or, does so through sports teams and athletic contests, a God, or other vehicle of the "other" beyond oneself through which the person's life gains illusory meaning.

Indeed, Becker saw that "transference represents the natural heroics striving for a 'beyond' that gives self-validation." He goes on to say: "As Rank so wisely saw, projection is a *necessary unburdening* of the individual...man ... must project the meaning of his life outward, the reason for it, even the blame for it."

The person comes to construct his LIE, by the psychological mechanism of transference or projection, through the socialization process. He learns the methods for obtaining heroism [via others, a God concept or myth, sports teams, romantic or sexual interests, among many other methods] from his parents, his interactions with others, the media, and a host of other socialization forces present in the culture onto which he transfers or projects his fear of his own creatureliness and death.

As Becker put it:

> ...And what does the whole growing up period signify, if not the giving over of one's life-project?...What we will see is that man cuts out for himself a manageable world: he throws himself into action uncritically, unthinkingly. He accepts the cultural programming that turns his nose where he is supposed to look...the result is that he comes to exist in the imagined

infallibility of the world around him. He doesn't have to have
fears when his feet are solidly mired and his life mapped out in
a ready-made maze. All he has to do is to plunge ahead in a
compulsive style of driven-ness in the "ways of the world" that
he child learns and in which he lives later as a kind of grim
equanimity…

In sum, humans are programmed by the socialization process present and acting in all cultures, to adopt a way of life, or life immortality elusion (LIE), as termed by this Manifesto, which enables him or her to deny or repress the reality of death. Thus, societies are predisposed to creating systems – which Becker termed, "hero systems" - which enable its members to strive for self-worth and universal meaning by constructing individual LIEs (which Becker termed the life immortality project) based largely on subjective, symbolic and illusory beliefs which have arisen and developed in the culture in which he or she lives. Through these cultural hero systems, humans are able to conquer their otherwise unbearable awareness of impending and eventual death and the meaningless of life in light of that stark reality.

(E). <u>The Nature of Hero Systems</u>

A hero system arises then from beliefs which have developed in a cultural group (family, tribe, gang, fraternal organization, nation, etc.) based upon its socio-economic, political and theological antecedents and their subsequent evolution. From those values or beliefs, action methods arise, are defined and developed, that guide the person's quest for attaining a level of self-esteem and help establish a connection to the promise of personal immortality. The typical cultural hero system thus consists of various methods, based upon the underlying beliefs in the culture, enabling the members of a cultural group to repress the terror of death's inevitability, and the consequent meaninglessness of existence which such inevitability imposes on the human psyche. Indeed, Becker recognized that "history can thus be looked at as a succession of immortality ideologies; or, as a mixture at any time of several of these ideologies."

Thus, a cultural hero system, by symbolic means and methods, makes individual existence meaningful, by enabling one to construct illusory life immortality projects (i.e., LIEs) which, for various reasons, infuse one's life with meaning and self-esteem. Cultural hero systems also provide its members with a sense of belonging to a universal purpose, a *Beyond,* which offers the promise of personal immortal salvation in some or other form of existence in an "afterlife," as well as establishing a connection to "God" and the Cosmos. The methods for attaining self-esteem and a sense of immortal purpose constitute the primary motivational forces in society. They are the mainsprings of human action.

All cultures offer the same following and non-exhaustive general assortment of beliefs giving rise to the action methods for becoming heroic – that is, for enabling the individual member of a culture to construct his or her life immortality elusion (LIE) directing his behavior in order to gain self-esteem and the promise of immortality to overcome the fear of death:

Beliefs	Action Methods for Attaining Self-Esteem/Personal Immortality
1. Religious:	Provides a supernatural cosmology, a definition for the God con-

cept, and His relationship with mankind, and rituals and a moral code regarding how one is to live one's life in order to gain immortality;

2. <u>Economic</u>: Concerns systems for the production and distribution of goods and services within and among cultural groups. Economic systems provide the various methods of employment and entrepreneurship that fulfill basic needs for food and shelter, while at the same time providing for an avenue for individual self-esteem in the construction of one's LIE. It also involves as a means to self-esteem the attachment to material wealth, also known as consumerism, especially in Western societies;

3. <u>Romantic</u>: Provides the individual with a means to self-esteem through physical and psychological attraction and attachment to another, that is, the love object;

4. <u>Familial</u>: Enables a person to initially find his or her place in the world by competition for love and materials among one's parents and siblings;

5. Leisure: Provides the individual with the means to self-esteem by participation in and observation (termed here, spectator-ism) of recreational or competitive amateur and professional athletics by watching television; engaging in hobbies; by playing computer games; and, by engaging in a multitude of other possible leisure activities;

6. Social: Provides self-esteem and connection to the beyond via relatioships and interactions outside the family structure;

7. Political: Engaging in personal or partisan political activity, or being drawn to and driven by a political leader or ideology furnishes individual self-esteem and connection with a greater beyond;

8. Artistic: Writing, music, visual arts, media arts, etc., provides the means to personal self-esteem;

9. Celebrity: Provides self-esteem by enabling the person to live vicariously by worshipping or celebrating others.

Hero systems are fluid and change from individual

to individual among cultures, or even within the same culture, depending on upbringing, personality, and random experience, but are all essentially made up from a combination of the above general categories of beliefs supplying death denial action stratagems for the individual to create his or her life immortality elusion (LIE) that motivates his or her conduct.

Using the above categories of beliefs, a person's life LIE, or life/immortality project, may be described by the following equation:

LIE = Religious + Economic + Romantic + Religious + Leisure + Social + Political + Artistic Beliefs = Individual Human Behavior.

Thus, a person's behavior is determined by actions stemming from the particular methods of heroism that have been selected by him or her to deny or hide the reality of death.

This leads to the following simplified equation which restates Becker's assertion that death is the mainspring of human action:

DEATH = LIFE (or LIE).

In summary, the prospect of death, and associated problem of the utter meaninglessness of life which that stark realization imposes on the human psyche, are repressed by the person's LIE, learned and constructed from the culture in which he or she was born and raised. Thus, a person's repression of the death/meaninglessness problem is achieved through his or her religious affiliation and the practice of religious ritual; occupation; by participating in the struggles and achievements of the family unit and by raising children, and by often gaining self-worth through the achievement of children; by participating in sports or other "recreational" activities or hobbies, or by engaging in spectator-ism, that is, the thrill of sports achievement vicariously through attendance at games and becoming a fan of a team or player; by falling in love; by engaging in sex; by joining various societal groups with various agendas and purposes (even street gangs); by creating "art;" and etcetera, etcetera, etcetera, *ad infinatum.*

(F). Religious Faith: The Need For God

By necessity, every culture has a religious component in its hero system which, through some sort of mythical or theological story, explains the creation of mankind and connection between the individual and species with God, as well as providing the means for gaining personal immortality in some definable afterlife. Thus, even in secular and materialistic cultures like America, religion plays a primary and important role in assisting the individual in overcoming the stark terror and finality of death.

As Becker put it:

… religion solves the problem of death, which no living individuals can solve, no matter how they would support us. Religion, then, gives the possibility of heroic victory in freedom and solves the problem of human dignity at its highest level. The two ontological motives of the human condition are both met: the need to surrender oneself in full to the rest of nature, to become a part of it by laying down one's whole existence to some higher meaning; and the need to expand oneself as an individual heroic personality.

- Becker, *The Denial of Death*, 203

Religion thus offers the individual with both the opportunity of becoming a meaningful presence in the present world by obeying the precepts and rituals of his or her religion, while also offering the promise of immorality in some definable afterlife as a direct, if not often simple-minded and naive, method for resolving the problem of the finality of life.

As Becker noted, it should not be surprising that the members of cultures like Soviet Russia, whose political ideology, communism, was strictly anti-religious thus downplaying and even forbidding a role of God in the lives of their citizens, were beset with psychological problems related directly to this prohibition. Likewise, the cold scientific world view which arose in the late 1800s, marked by the publication of Darwin's *On the Origin of Species*, that diminished the ability of religious belief to provide a credible cosmological explanation for the universe and afterlife, caused many to experience a serious and damaging psychological quandary. The rise of science which tore down old religious beliefs in the nature of the universe and God's relationship with it, and the human species He created, has engendered a spiritual chasm which modern scientific theory has been unable to bridge despite recent efforts in scientific literature to link science, though the oddness of quantum mechanics, and spirituality. However, unlike the cosmologies of the old religions, modern science does not present an easy and comprehensible definition of God and the nature of the Universe, or provide a definitive means to personal immortality.

In sum, in order to overcome the death anxiety, all human cultures, through religion, provide their constituents with an explanation, or myth, for God's existence and interaction with the human race, including what happens to the "soul" or persona after the individual dies. However, because such explanations largely depend on the concept of blind "faith" scientific advances in the modern era have greatly diminished the ability of those constituents to believe in the myths established by what are now ancient and intellectually discredited religions.

Thus, it has become difficult, if not impossible, for the educated modern man to reconcile his understanding of the universe, as described and demonstrated by the advances and discoveries of science, with the old myths of a personal God intermeddling with human society as described in the Old and New Testaments, the Koran, Torah, or other ancient holy books. Nor does the description of a secular, indifferent God of the Enlightenment provide modern human beings with a needed relief from their immortal longing, from their incessant need to find an answer to death.

At present, therefore, mankind is at a cross-roads of faith. We can either find "blind faith" in some false cosmic construct of God to fill the gap, or select a true path to an understanding of the Universe, and, therefore, God. Such path, as offered by the Genuine Hero System proposed by this Manifesto, does not depend on mere "blind" faith, but on real action by the incessant pursuit of examination and discovery in order to reveal a genuine understanding of the true nature of God and the Cosmos.

(G). Summary: Constructing the LIE From Hero Systems

The individual's Life Immortality Elusion (LIE) is a direct result of the hero system of the culture in which the individual resides. It is constructed from the methods offered by the culture for satisfying the person's urge for meaning and special-ness (self-esteem), and from the religious beliefs offered by the cultural group that enables the person to establish a connection with God, the Cosmos and immortality in some definable and mythical afterlife. Through these culture mechanisms, humans achieve both meaning and immortal purpose. Indeed, as Becker argued, "it is culture itself that embodies the transcendence of death in some form or other, whether it appears purely religious or not...culture itself is sacred, since *it* is the 'religion' that assures in some way the perpetuation of its members."

The personal construction of one's LIE is derived from the socialization process in the culture in which the person resides. Self-esteem is thus wholly culturally dependent and learned.

As noted by Solomon, Greenberg, and Pyszczynski in their article, <u>Tales From the Crypt: On the Role of Death in Life</u> :

> *Preparation for this transition begins during socialization, as childrenlearn the ways of the world suffused through their culture's history, religion,and folklore... although self-esteem is an individual psychologicalattribute, it is ultimately culturally constructed in that there is nostraightforward way to feel good about oneself in the absence of socially prescribed standards of right and wrong; and there are consequently noabsolute and transcendental standards by which human beings can ever differentiate between good and evil.*

Furthermore, the LIE is culturally relativistic and, even in the same culture, can exhibit infinitely various modes. Personal reality is thus different depending not only on the culture in which one resides historically and physically, but on the various methods employed within the same culture, based upon the process of individual socialization for constructing one's LIE.

Solomon, Greenberg and Pyszczynski support the

idea of the relativism of cultural constructed LIEs, and further recognize that the very relativism of cultural reality creation explains in large measure the often violent conflict and clash of cultures:

> ... *just as the standards by which self-esteem is acquired are arbitrary in that they vary across time and space, so too are cultural worldviews arbitrary in that there is a potentially infinite variety of cultural worldviews that have existed, do exist, or could conceivably exist, each of which is believed by the average enculturated individual to be an absolute representation of reality.*

> ...*this conceptual analysis helps us understand why human beings have such a difficult time peacefully coexisting with different others. To the extent that cultural worldviews serve to ameliorate the anxiety associated with the awareness of death, the mere existence of others who have different beliefs about the nature of reality poses an explicit challenge to the claims of absolute truth of one's own point of view, thus undermining the anxiety-buffering capacity of that worldview and instigating defensive responses that serve to restore psychological equanimity through the acquisition of a new cultural worldview or enhanced allegiance to the original worldview.*
> - Tales From the Crypt: On the Role of Death in Life

Human discord can therefore be largely explained by the differences among cultural view systems for providing their members with self-esteem and a connection to God, in the construction of individual LIEs. The historic clash between Christianity and Islam is a glaring example of this ancient and prevalent discord, but it is also evident in almost all manner of group versus group confrontation. We fear other groups, at bottom, because their beliefs may render our own obsolete, or insignificant and insufficient, thus diminishing the symbolic "truth" of our LIE in the quest of alleviating the death/meaningless anxiety which hounds our individual lives. Of course, this in turn would lay bare the fact that we are mere flesh and blood creatures destined for death. Thus, we are compelled to fight to the death to diminish the culture of another that conflicts with the methods of constructing LIEs in our own.

(H). The Inauthentic and Neurotic Man

Heroic action systems have developed in cultural groups as a consequence of the death terror which our superior intelligence has imposed upon the human psyche. Each culture offers the means and methods, stemming from its core socio-economic, political and religious beliefs, for the construction of life immortality elusions, of LIEs, which are the motivational forces for attaining individual self-esteem, and for realizing a connection to a concept of God, the Cosmos and personal supernatural immortality. Culture is thus a vehicle for creating personal reality, the LIE of human existence.

As recognized by Kierkegaard, most individuals become a slave to the symbolic methods offered by culture in constructing their respective LIEs in an futile attempt to overcome death. Such "automatic cultural man," as Becker called him, "imagines that he has an identity if he pays his insurance premium...guns his sports car or works his electric toothbrush."

But even worse, these cultural offerings may ultimately blind the individual to the reality of his earthly condition. As Becker put it: "Man is protected by the secure and limited alternatives his society offers him, and if he does not look up from his path he can live out his life with a certain dull certainty."

And even beyond that, though the symbolic cultural heroic methods may allow the individual to forget the fact that they are flesh and blood creatures who eat other creatures, piss, shit and ultimately die, the end result are human cultural groups which inflict violence on other cultural groups and ultimately fail to lead mankind to the highest level of achievement. Perhaps such blinding of reality could be forgiven in some small way if it at least led to a species to advanced technologies and the promise of eternal survival instead of the present one that seems incapable of escaping from the violent and wasteful spiral of warfare, ignorance and poverty.

Becker further noted that "the essence of normality is the refusal of reality." Neurosis is thus universal. We are all neurotic in some sense. However, as Becker also reflected: "Some people have more trouble with their lies than others." He went on to say: "But we can also see at once that there is no line between normal and neurotic, as we all lie and are all bound in some ways by the lies. Neurosis is, then, something we all share; it is universal."

A man becomes aware of his neurosis, as Becker further stated, "when his lie begins to show the damaging effects on him or the people around him and he seeks clinical help for it – or others seek it for him. Otherwise, we call the refusal of reality 'normal' because it doesn't occasion any visible problems."

The person who abides by the methods offered by his culture for denying death and constructs a LIE in conformance therewith, is deemed sane. He goes about his business like his fellow cultural members – shows up to work on time, does his job more or less competently, and engages in the other methods of self-esteem creation with various levels of success, and even attends his church regularly – and he is thus deemed a "normal" or well-adjusted person. However, he is in truth denying the obvious reality of his existence that none of his actions matter in the face of death and his creatureliness. His life work is a mere symbolic, ultimately meaningless denial of that reality. And deep down, he realizes this and this realization causes varying degrees of psychological pain and sometimes, dysfunctional conduct.

Although the problem of death has been resolved historically, and in the present world, through the mechanism of cultural hero systems, as will be further developed in the next chapter, because they are defective and insufficient in a basic sense, and often conflict with each other in primal ways, historic and modern heroic action systems have failed to resolve the death/meaningless terror in the minds of men; have resulted in destructive and useless human behavior within and without the cultural hero system; and, are the ultimate cause for the stunting of mankind's growth. In sum, the failure of hero systems explains the human species' failure to attain its spiritual, intellectual and technological potential. Or, as Becker so bleakly put it: "...man's natural and inevitable urge to deny mortality and achieve a heroic self-image are the root causes of human evil."

Let us in the next chapter explore those root causes and the damaging effects of the methods employed by mankind in the quest to deny his reality.

CHAPTER THREE
THE FAILURE OF
CULTURAL HERO SYSTEMS

Welfare rolls, alcoholism, drug addition, suicide rates,
highway fatalities, the so-called breakdown of moral fiber –
all attest to a society which, for too many, does not offer
the means to a satisfactory expression of purpose...
The societal breakdown is largely due, I believe,
to a state of transition in which we, as a culture,
find ourselves. We move from the 19th century purposes
which are no longer relevant in the latter part of the 20th century,
to 21st century purposes which are not yet in place.
- Barbara Dewey

It is fateful and ironic how the lie we need in order to live
dooms us to a life that is never really ours.
- Ernest Becker

(A). <u>Introduction</u>
      There is no disputing that past and present cultural
hero systems have failed humanity in reaching its spiritual,

intellectual and technological potential. All one needs to do in support of this bleak assertion is to review any tome on the history of the human race, or pick up a newspaper anywhere on the planet, to realize how dismally our cultural hero systems have failed us. Mankind's legacy to date is constant warfare and violence, financial distress, poverty, sickness, ignorance, and the general failure of imagination.

The explanation for such failure of achievement is that the cultural hero systems devised to date have furnished inadequate means for attaining individual self-esteem, and/or a connection with the universal Beyond by failing to accurately conceptualize God and the Cosmos; or, that past and present cultural hero systems do so in ways that are inimical to the individual and collective human good, or that are inconsequential toward attaining those lofty and reasonable goals.

This failure is explainable, in part, due to the fact that the beliefs making up historic and modern cultural symbolic hero systems, especially religious beliefs, are largely, if not entirely, based upon "un-reality," or pure myth – that is, a conceptualization of nature and existence, and mankind's place in it, which is seriously flawed if not utterly mistaken. Deep down in the subconscious realm, humans recognize the fallacy of the myths cultures employ in offering methods of heroism upon which their life illusions required to deny death are based. Stated another way, culture fails to adequately resolve the problem of the human condition that tirelessly haunts our waking hours and our dreams: that we are defecating creatures doomed to die. As Becker wrote: "The fact is that self-transcendence via culture does not give man a simple and straight-forward solution to the problem of death; the terror of death still rumbles underneath the cultural repression." Thus, the individuals go about their daily lives dissatisfied and full of dread with death rumbling constantly beneath the surface of conscious thought and everyday action. It thus haunts the individual with constant anxiety and dread, and is the root cause for numerous mental disorders and worse, for evil itself.

Moreover, the very methods offered by cultures to its members to repress the idea of death have resulted in the pursuit of activities that have been unproductive or counter-productive to enhancing the qualify of life for a considerable number of human beings and have also stunted the achievement of human spiritual, intellectual and technological progress and potential; have failed to ensure the survival of the species; and, have led to false or skewered conceptualizations of God and the Cosmos. Indeed, many of the activities motivated by the methods for attaining heroism in cultures are destructive and appear to be hastening, as Becker feared, mankind's seemingly inevitable road to extinction.

As recognized by the philosopher, Soren Kierkegaard, as well as Becker, there is only one reality which we human beings need admit and accept: that each of us is a flesh-and-blood creature destined to die; and, that what we are driven to do based upon the hero system offered by the culture in which we live – that is, the LIE we have constructed from the methods of heroism offered by our culture - means absolutely nothing in light of the stark fact of death.

Moreover, the realization and acceptance of this simple yet profoundly important idea will set the individual free to develop what is essential to human psychological health and fulfillment – that is, an authentic sense of what acts are truly important to the develop of genuine self-esteem, as well as true faith in God based upon the reality of existence, and the fact of death, and not upon false myth.

(B). <u>The Historical Failure of Cultural Hero Systems</u>

Becker recognized that in "primitive" societies, individuals are motivated to action that is almost exclusively designed to help the group or tribe survive, or for the purpose of procreation. Thus, heroic behavior is based upon actual betterment of one's own and one's neighbors lives, as well as the survival of the tribe (and by that act, the species). In such cultures, there is little time to do anything else except gather food, construct shelters, avoid dangers, nurture young and train them in tribal survival techniques, procreate, engage in rudimentary rituals that recognize the importance of cooperation and affection among tribal members, and do all the other things in a concerted effort to enhance one's own survival as well as the survival of one's tribe. As Becker put it: "For primitive man, who practiced the ritual renewal of nature, each person could be a cosmic hero of a quite definite kind: he could contribute with his powers and observances to the replenishment of cosmic life."

However, with the rise of "civilizations" following the agricultural revolution some 6,000 to 10,000 years ago, helping the tribe or group survive was no longer the primary, if not sole, activity and occupation for individuals. In these agrarian, civilized societies, heroism necessarily had to take a different path. Indeed, the heroism of a farmer is quite different than that of a hunter-gatherer. The new civilized cultures thus developed symbolic hero systems offering new methods for alleviating the death/meaninglessness anxiety resulting from the awareness of death. A new cosmology evolved that was grounded outside the environment, as it had been for the primitive, nomadic hunters, and became tuned to the divine. As Becker recognized: "Gradually as societies became more complex and differentiated into classes, cosmic heroism became the property of special classes like divine kings and the military, who were charged with the renewal of nature and the protection of the group by means of their own special powers."

Moreover, a by-product of agrarian civilization was the vast increase of leisure time. The inhabitants of these advanced cultures used this additional time to more fully and directly contemplate the human condition - existence, death, the nature of reality, and the concept of God. In short, to philosophize and to engage in play in its many guises. Indeed, the kings and priesthoods of ancient civilizations were founded and gained power and control based upon the contemplation of the supernatural world and the gods, and the resulting cosmological explanations which such contemplations necessary evoked.

Perhaps the phenomenon of the megaliths which exploded around the world, and especially in the British Isles, between 6000-4000 BCE, best exemplifies this sudden concentration of human thought and contemplation on death and the other-worldly realm, resulting from the agricultural revolution and rise of settled communities culminating in the first advanced civilizations of Sumer and Egypt. This seeming single-minded and obsessive dedication to the construction of gigantic stone edifices (e.g., Stonehenge) as symbolic representations of, and homage to God and/ or the Cosmos, or at very least some mythic or psychic force beyond the comprehension of the humans constructing them, was the direct result of the expansion of leisure time which enabled the rulers and priests of these civilizations to consider the profound cosmological, philosophical and theological questions now confronting them, such as the creation of the universe and human species, God's role in it and His relation to humanity, and, of course, of existence and death.

Such leisure time, naturally, became concentrated in the ruling classes, and the priesthoods which arose in these early agrarian societies, who were often one and the same. As Roger Osborne dourly noted in *Civilization: A New History of the Western World*: "A life of intermittent hunting and rest was exchanged for one of unremitting toil, which enabled more people to live together but benefited only those with power over these lower groups." With perhaps too much time now to contemplate the inevitability of death, the ruling classes/priesthoods soon developed whole cosmologies explaining existence and the role of God in it, the meaning of life, and the means to gain personal immortality. A by-product of such pronouncements, which eventually themselves became seen as divine proclamations, was control over the masses through moral codes based upon God's relationship to the culture and to the king or ruler making the pronouncements. Indeed, as communists have postulated, religion has always been a convenient tool used by the ruling classes, encompassing the few, to reign over the many leading to Marx' famous saying that religion is the opium of the masses, deadening them intellectually to the true nature of their plight. (This phenomenon – the need to be led by a charismatic person of divine connection, Becker argued, was yet further proof of the individual's need to attach himself to a particular leader, group, or creed, to follow with the masses, if you will, some messenger or credo, in order to repel the terror of death). Indeed, humanity has always been organized as an oligarchy under different guises.

As history has demonstrated, almost all the early, and later, contemplations regarding the nature of the God and the Cosmos, and the various myths that rose up around them, have been "proven" by successive cosmologies and, of course, by modern science, to have been flat out wrong. As human civilizations rose and declined and, religious and theological dogmas changed or were replaced, new explanations regarding the nature of God and the Cosmos, and mankind's interaction with them, were offered and accepted upon faith, and on and on until modern times. Indeed, over the long centuries of human history, certain similarities arose among religious concepts, which Karl Jung has term, archetypes, starting with the ancient Epic of Gilgamesh, grandly and epically interrupting the role and meaning of death in the lives of men.

However, the aim of each religion in every past and present culture has remained constant – to provide an explanation for death and offer the promise of personal immortality in some kind of definable afterlife. (There are exceptions, such as ancient Egyptian cosmologies, which had no real place for the common man in an immortal afterlife). As shall be argued in succeeding chapters, the problem has always been that religion has never been able to satisfactorily and completely prove to its adherents that the God described in its dogma exists, that He or She is interested in the society of mankind, and that He or She offers a place of residence in an afterlife of some kind for individuals who have already died, and who, like you and this writer, are yet destined for death.

Likewise, the Cosmos – the physical world around us, has been explained in myriad complex ways over the march of human history since those ancient times, and in each epoch the prior version of the nature of physical reality has been debunked or expanded upon by successive scientific studies. The Aristotelian and Ptolemaic cosmology, placing earth at the center of the universe, so avidly adopted by the Catholic Church, was replaced by the cosmologies of Copernicus, Galileo, and Kepler, placing instead the sun at the center of the solar system. Later discoveries demonstrated that the solar system inhabited by humans is a mere speck in a vast universe which, it is estimated, is 15 billion years old. Until today, we are faced with a complex view of nature with some theories proclaiming that there may be ten or eleven dimensions and parallel versions of ourselves and that matter, the stuff of the universe, planets, stars, ourselves, is made up of strings connected in some strange way to some universal force which as of yet remains undiscovered.

The point of this review of the progression of changed understandings of natural reality, and the premise of this Manifesto, is that since cultural hero systems are necessarily products of current theological and cosmological understanding, they have consistently been deficient in important respects because they are based on a lack of full comprehension, and hence myth, rather than on the genuine or true nature of physical and spiritual reality and existence. The LIE, indeed, is and has always been, based upon a lie regarding the nature of Nature and of God and the Cosmos. Therefore, culture has provided methods for constructing LIEs which are necessarily false, and recognized as such deep down in the psyche by each member of the respective historical culture.

Thus, mankind must come to the realization that the hero systems, and the beliefs underlying them, which have arisen among past and present cultures are inherently flawed, and upon reaching and acknowledging that significant epiphany, discard them and adopt a global Genuine Hero System, based as it is on the "known" or genuinely and currently understood reality, as the motivational force for human behavior.

Succeeding chapters shall more fully explore the falsity of specific beliefs of historic and modern cultural hero systems in explaining the failure of such systems to provide relief to the individual and the species from the death/meaningless anxiety, and hence result in the failure of the species to attain its highest potential in all areas of endeavor.

(C). The Inauthentic Man

Historic and modern cultural hero systems thus fail in three primary respects:

1. They inadequately resolve the death/meaninglessness dilemma in the individual's psyche, and thus render the person without sufficient self-esteem, and hence unfulfilled and unhappy;

2. They lead to "inauthentic" individuals, who engage in actions almost mindlessly, and the result is inconsequential or trivial behavior; and/or

3. They lead to destructive behavior.

The ultimate result of such failure is a species doomed to extinction, as worried Becker, and certainly one that fails to achieve its potential.

It was Henry David Thoreau who said that men go about their lives in "quiet desperation." Life is dreadful because deep down each of us, some more than others, recognize that what we are doing in our everyday lives do not gain us what we seek – escape from our fear of death. What we do is ultimately meaningless because we die. We may live through our children, as the means of genetic proliferation, but hardly is that something we would find fetching or satisfying if etched onto our tombstones.

To Kierkegaard, however, having some sentience of the dread of death is better than none at all. He despaired of the "inauthentic" man, that person so wrapped up in his LIE that he is forever blinded from the truth and reality of his existence and condition. As Becker clarified the point:

> They are "inauthentic" in that they do not belong to themselves, are not "their own" person, do not act from their own center, do not see reality on it terms; they are one-dimensional men totally immersed in the fictional games being played in their society, unable to transcend their social conditioning: the corporation men of the West, the bureaucrats of the East, the tribal men locked up in tradition – man everywhere who doesn't understand what it means to think for himself and who, if he did, would shrink back at the idea of such audacity and exposure.

The Genuine Hero System proposed by this *Manifesto* turns that worry on its head, and proposes a society which fully and passionately embraces the human condition – the reality of death – as its guiding principle for the formation of beliefs that will inspire and direct human action and behavior. The result is the hoped for creation of the genuine, or to use a Kierkegaardian term – an authentic man.

(D). The Genuine Hero System

Becker postulated that "if everyone admitted his urge to be a hero...it would make men demand that culture give them their due...a primary sense of human value as unique contributors to cosmic life." He further argued: "Only those societies we today call 'primitive' provided this feeling for their members."

This Manifesto urges humans to make that audacious demand of their respective cultures, that they give them "a primary sense of human value as unique contributors to cosmic life." In short, we should demand that society be structured in a way that offers genuine relief from the terror of death, not some illusory, symbolic project that serves only to obscure rather than actually overcome it, and worse still, fails to serve the individual and collective good. As Becker realized, the failure of human societies to answer this demand will result in the inevitable and eventual extinction of the human species.

This Manifesto offers more than the mere recommendation that its readers abandon their LIEs, but also offers a blueprint for the establishment of a "genuine" hero system, global in scope and content, to act as the motivating force behind human behavior that like "primitive" societies, individually and collectively contributes to a practical and philosophical purpose. In short, it is based on the belief that doing good works for, and bettering the lives of other human beings, and contributing to the survival of the species will enable the individual to attain a genuine kind of self-esteem that will enable him to construct a LIE that will genuinely obscure the prospect of death.

This genuine cultural hero system is based upon the further belief that human beings have the potential to comprehend and become God-like, if not one with some kind of Cosmic Force. The main "religious" component of the genuine hero system is that there exists a supernatural force and entity that transcends the physical universe which, at this juncture in our spiritual, intellectual and technological development, we are simply and unfortunately unable to comprehend; and, therefore, we must embark upon a scientific and spiritual quest for such comprehension.

Adopting these beliefs as the motivational, heroic forces underlying the conduct of mankind will direct action that is beneficial to the individual and collective quality of life; will enhance the survivability of the species; and, will lead to a comprehension of God and the Cosmos. Together these pursuits may alleviate Becker's fear that mankind is doomed to extinction.

Individual and group survival has always been perilous and dependent upon profound natural forces beyond the control of the person or group within which he or she lives.

No one can reasonably argue against the proposition that, unless mankind advances technologically far beyond its current stage, it is doomed to become extinct due to, among other things, some tragic environmental event, such as an asteroid or comet impacting the earth, or the sudden onset of some exotic plague. With our present disharmonious world governmental structure, it is just as likely that we will destroy ourselves with weapons of mass destruction. And as the astronomers tell us, even should we somehow avoid obliteration by one or another of these natural or artificial means, we are destined to be destroyed, albeit billions of years in the future, when the sun expands in its inevitable course of stellar evolution and demise.

In short, as stated at the outset of this Manifesto, unless we become much more spiritually, intellectually, and technologically advanced than we have to date, after 100,000 years of existence as a distinctly human species, humanity is doomed to certain extinction at some uncertain date - whether it be tomorrow or a million or billion years hence - in the future. That doom is certain, *unless and until*, a system of belief, organization and government is developed and adopted based upon survival of the species, and achievement of a comprehension of existence and the cosmic God, as its primary goals.

Indeed, as Becker recognized – the survival of the human animal through vast eons would be a hollow victory if not accompanied by some meaningful reason for achieving such magnificent longevity. The goal of species survival must therefore be accompanied by the quest for a comprehension of God through technological, intellectual and spiritual pursuit and advancement as the concomitant point of it.

In summary, the Genuine Hero System will arise only from a society whose members adopt as their *raison d'être* the ultimate survival of the human species together with the intellectual and spiritual effort to know God.

CHAPTER FOUR
THE FAILURE OF RELIGION

...[Freud] says religion is a danger because it
tends to sanctify bad human institutions with which
it has allied itself throughout its history;
further, by teaching people to believe in an illusion
and by prohibiting critical thinking, religion is
responsible for the impoverishment of human intelligence.
- Erich Fromm

(A). Introduction: The General Failure of Religious Belief
(1). Commonalities Among Historic and Modern Religious Belief Systems

Throughout human history, religious belief has been an essential method offered by cultural hero systems to their members for overcoming and repressing the fear of death. Religion satisfies the basic needs of the individual of establishing a connection to a God concept and an afterlife – a supernatural place where the person's soul travels once the physical body decays and dies. Thus, all religions offer a description of God and the promise of personal immortality as an essential answer to the human condition.

Numerous and varied, and sometimes bizarre, theologies have arisen in historical and present cultures. No matter how diverse or strange, however, each establishes a direct and tangible connection to God and the supernatural afterlife. Personal immortality is guaranteed if the individual adherent of a particular religion follows certain spiritual guidelines and duties outlined in its theological matrix that has developed as dogma over time. They also offer cultural members with another avenue for obtaining personal self-esteem by following certain set mores or rules of behavior. Such mores or rules often constitute a kind of legal code that also serves the important purpose of establishing appropriate behavioral parameters among individuals in a group. Thus, religion has also been seen as a socializing tool in bringing the group together for the pursuit of common survival needs by regulating behavior. The Ten Commandments of early Judaism clearly illustrate this legislative component of religious doctrine. Indeed, certain of the Commandments proscribing murder, theft, and bearing false witness remain part of modern penal codes.

However, as Becker postulated, the primary function of religious belief is to satisfy the need for individuals to establish a connection with the supernatural "beyond," the realm outside the reality of physical existence perceived through the five senses. Religions do that by supplying the individual with a description or vision of a "God" concept, or a cosmological characterization. This characterization is universal in scope, and invariably includes an explanation for creation of the human species, how the deity or deities have become divinely and directly involved in the Cosmos and in the course of human affairs. Lastly, all religions provide an explanation for the purpose and meaning of death to the individual and the species.

All human religious creeds thus provide their adherents with a prescription for salvation and immortality in a definable afterlife through a belief in God or gods residing in His, or sometimes, Her, cosmic, supernatural realm. In this way, religions enable individuals to establish the needed connection to some *Beyond,* to a God Concept, as a means to personal immortality. In short, the religious belief of a cultural group provides the individual member of that cultural group with supernatural meaning outside, and in addition to, the physical realm through the promise of salvation in the afterlife envisioned by the religion about whose theological precepts and dogma the individual has gained a measure of belief and faith through the socialization process. Thus, religious belief, in a direct and emotionally charged way, provides the individual with a comprehensible and obtainable method for directly overcoming and denying death.

Through the institutions of family, friendship, education, and media, the socialization process programs individual cultural members with the basic underlying precepts and cosmological view of the religious belief for that culture, and the codes of conduct required by that belief. In short, individuals of a culture adopt its religious beliefs normally because they are raised – that is, programmed - to do so. The realization of Faith in the religious creed, derived from the socialization process, provides the individual with the methods for attaining self-esteem by following religious codes establishing a direct path to personal divine immortality. Thus, the idea of unreasoning and unquestioning faith in religious belief offered by culture becomes an anchor for the individual's death denial response. One gains a link to immortality through religious faith, and thus, release from the awful prospect of oblivion and meaninglessness which the inevitability of death inspires in the human psyche.

(2). How Religious Belief Motivates Violent and Destructive Behavior

There is no question that religion has been a primary factor motivating human destructive behavior and warfare among human cultural groups. Such violent conflicts are sparked by the different ways religious myths which have arisen in those groups define God and the nature of the Cosmos and often conflict with each other. The motivation to fight and destroy whole peoples who embrace a way to God and personal immortality via a different supernatural and religious cosmology from one's own is related to the fact that such contrary theological viewpoint negates one's own, and hence destroys or leaves open to serious question one's promise of personal immortality.

Thus, the mere challenge to a culture's religious theology by another culture's religion, or even by individuals within the same culture who dare to question the core beliefs of such theology, causes the faithful members of the culture to become intensely and sometimes insanely insecure and defensive, and then sometimes irrationally violent. If such faith is profoundly shaken, as it has been in modern times due to the momentous expansion of scientific understanding, the shaken believer may become depressed, deranged or lost.

The debate among competing beliefs regarding the nature of God is often heated and virulent. As noted by social scientists, Sheldon Solomon, Jeff Greenberg, and Tom Pyszczynski, in Tales From the Crypt: On the Role of Death in Life:

To the extent that cultural worldviews serve to ameliorate the anxiety associated with the awareness of death, the mere existence of others who have different beliefs about the nature of reality poses an explicit challenge to the claims of absolute truth of one's own point of view, thus undermining the anxiety-buffering capacity of that worldview and instigating defensive responses that serve to restore psychological equanimity through the acquisition of a new cultural worldview or enhanced allegiance to the original worldview.

In short, contrary explanations for God and Cosmic existence, the creation of the Universe, Life, and the afterlife, are usually fanatically and violently opposed because they tend to render one's version of God and Cosmic reality, and the possibility of supernatural immortality, inconsequential or false, thus exposing the person to the full psychological onslaught of the stark reality of death and the meaningless of life. This is no more evident than in the historical battle which has raged for over 1400 years between the Christian and Islamic faithful. It has likewise manifested itself in the historic violent struggles between the Hindu and Buddhist faithful.

The challenge to one's fundamental basis to faith exposes the possibility that he or she is a mere creature doomed to death without an otherworldly explanation that infuses one's life with sacred meaning and immortal purpose The negation of the promise of immortality is something that the human mind and psyche resists at all costs.

However, in the modern world, the essence of the reality of nature and the universe is being starkly altered almost daily through scientific examination and discovery; and that reality is in clear opposition to the description offered by the old religions. Thus, the dogmas of the old religions for the representation of God and the Cosmos are being directly challenged and in large measure, debunked.

Indeed, over the last two hundred fifty years, the advance of scientific knowledge has whittled away the foundational bases for the old religions underlying historical and modern cultural hero systems. Although hardly acknowledged, science has demonstrated again and again that the myths upon which the historic and traditional religions, such as Christianity and Islam, are based have falsely, or inaccurately, described the "God" concept and the Cosmos. And yet, despite these clear discoveries, such religions persist as an option in our cultural hero systems as a method to repress the death/meaninglessness anxiety.

In some respects, it was easier living in simpler times, before the advent and publication of various modern scientific theories, such as General and Special Relativity, the Big Bang Theory, and more recently, the various notions of String Theory, and other fantastical though coldly scientific (at least to the ordinary layman) ideas about the structure of matter and energy in the universe via quantum physics that have eclipsed or certainly obscured the idea of God as a Being having direct involvement or any relevancy for that matter in the course of human affairs.

As Becker pointed out:

Once we realize what the religious solution did, we can see how modern man edged himself into an impossible situation. He still needed to feel heroic, to know that his life mattered in the scheme of things; he still had to be specially "good" for something truly special. Also, he had to merge himself with some higher, self-absorbing meaning, in trust and in gratitude – what we saw as the universal motive of the Agape-merger. If he no longer had God, how was he to do this?

- Becker, <u>The Denial of Death</u>. p.160.

In other words, the attack on the basis for religious belief inspired by modern scientific discovery has undermined the individual's ability to fashion a connection to a supernatural "beyond;" and, thus has also resulted in a direct attack on the individual's ability to construct a reasoned basis for his own self-esteem in the eternal quest to repress the reality of death through faith in a rational God connected with his life. This is because the scientific "God" is coldly impersonal, and does not have involvement in human affairs. At best, among many scientists, he is seen as the cold intelligence behind the design of the universe. But to many, he is like a watchmaker who cares little for his product once it is produced and sold. God may be behind the cold mechanistic workings of the Universe, but He is without regard to the human species, or any species.

It is also not surprising then that challenges to religious dogma have always been met with fierce opposition from the religious hierarchy. Thus, the revolutionary theories of great scientific minds of the Renaissance, such as Copernicus and Galileo, garnered stern condemnation from the Roman Catholic Church. And even today, emotionally charged debates rage between those who champion evolution on the one side, and the creationists on the other; and, between the Intelligent Design theorists, and those who espouse the idea that the Cosmos has come to its present state not by some Devine plan, but based upon the cold laws of nature.

These conflicts seem to boil down to a fight between ideas for and against the existence of God. But without God, we are left with no way of connecting to something beyond the physical realm, and hence something beyond death. Thus, our connection to the possibility of immortality is broken without the existence of God, and hence the fervor of the debate.

Based upon the advance of human knowledge, it has been readily demonstrated that all religions are based upon artificial, inaccurate and/or incomplete cosmologies; that is, conceptualizations of God, existence, the universe, and the afterlife that are simply wrong because they were constructed from superstition and a lack of understanding of science. They are untrue, based upon illogic, fiction, falsehood, mere stories, pure myth and speculation, in a futile, silly and childish attempt to provide the believer with a connection to God and immortality that usually falls far on the other side of truth.

Furthermore, except for the most unreasoning and fanatical adherents, human beings living in the modern world have either admitted to themselves, or at least come to suspect, that the respective religious beliefs offered by their cultures do not accurately describe the nature of God and the Cosmos, and are instead based upon fiction or myth that is cosmologically inaccurate. In short, there is an at least implicit recognition in most humans that their understanding of God and immortality relies on false myth and is thus flawed.

However the hero systems among modern cultures lack a viable substitute explanation for God, Cosmic existence, the afterlife, and immortality, and thus are unable to provide an authentic, believable method for attaining a connection to some discernible *Beyond* sufficient to enable the individual to repress the fear of death. Without faith in the kind of afterlife and immortality offered by the religions among modern cultures, the member of that culture is left only to ponder the meaningless of existence. Hence, the desperate and pitiful resort to other methods of death denial offered by societies, such as militarism, fanaticism, spectator-ism, cultism, sex and romantic love addiction, substance abuse, and other addictions. These methods of self-esteem creation motivate the individual to violent or trivial behavior adverse to the individual or collective good equally as bad as actions motivated by religious faith. Of course, many still continue to rely on the old religious dogmas which provide more and more a sense of comfort in the idea of reality which they espouse, or whose message is altered to conform to modern scientific theory regarding the nature of the universe in a tortured effort to bring theology in line with an accurate description of reality.

The shortcomings of false religious myths extend beyond an inability to adequately define God, and the related failure to satisfy mankind's urge to repress the knowledge of death through Cosmic identification. As noted above, the human urge to religious belief also fosters violence in the defense of Faith, or to an effort to impose it upon the Faithless.

A slew of popular books each with a provocative anti-religious message have been published in recent years making this exact point – that is, arguing that religion has been and continues to be detrimental to individual fulfillment and human advancement. In disparaging faith in God, while championing the idea of atheism, or lack of belief in a God directly involved in human affairs (which appears in itself to be a kind of "belief" undertaken by these authors in the pursuit of their own heroic life immortality elusions), these books point out that faith in false religious myths is responsible for centuries of war, pillage, ignorance and poverty that has maimed or destroyed literally billions of human beings, and repressed the quality of life for billions more over at least 6000 years of recorded history.

In The God Delusion, for instance, Richard Dawkins gives this rather bleak assessment and summary of the results of the past two thousand years of religious faith:

> *The oldest of the three Abrahamic religions, and the clear ancestor of the other two, is Judaism: originally a tribal cult of a single fiercely unpleasant God, morbidly obsessed with sexual restrictions, with the smell of charred flesh, with his own superiority over rival gods and with the exclusiveness of his chosen desert tribe. During the Roman occupation of Palestine, Christianity was founded by Paul of Tarsus as a less ruthlessly monotheistic sect of Judaism and less exclusive one, which looked outwards from the Jews to the rest of the world. Several centuries later, Muhammad and his followers reverted to the uncompromising monotheism of the Jewish original, but not its exclusiveness, and found Islam upon a new holy book, the Koran, or Qur'an, adding a powerful ideology of military conquest to spread the faith. Christianity, too, was spread by the sword, wielded first by Roman hands after the Emperor Constantine raised it fro eccentric cult to official religion, then by Crusaders, and later by the conquistadores and other European invaders and colonists, with missionary accompaniment.*

Likewise, in <u>The End of Faith</u>, Sam Harris argues that because "intolerance is thus intrinsic to every creed," religious faith engenders violence between and even among believers. (As explained above, this intolerance can be directly traced to the threat posed by contrary theologies to the death denial prerogative of a person's own religious faith). In a similar vein, internationally renowned lecturer, teacher and psychologist, James Hillman recognized that religion is often the motivating force behind destructive behavior and war among men. In <u>A Terrible Love of War</u>, he wrote:

The religions of Yahweh, Allah, and God the Father, with all their twiggy denominations, are sister branches of the one monotheistic root of which each claims to be the one and only true daughter. All place Abraham/Ibrahim among the founding patriarchs, and all point to his willingness to kill his son for the sake of the common god as an exemplary lesson. All regard Jerusalem as their own holy city. All still declare that their god is compassionate and have been killing one another for centuries. Of course Jesus is not divine for the other two and Mohammed is not a prophet for the other two, but they all begin in the Bible, grew first in the same religion-bearing earth of the Middle East, and have strength of monotheism in common. But the commitment to the singleness of vision that monotheism inflicts has them each inflicting centuries of terror on one another, and even on others in distant lands not concerned with their god or their disputes.

In conclusion, history has amply demonstrated that religious belief results in behavior that is adverse to human progress and individual fulfillment and happiness, and that is often destructive. This is because the underlying theologies of most, if not all, past and present religions inaccurately or falsely define God and the Universe in its cosmological underpinnings; and because the individual is unable to psychologically tolerate views inconsistent with his or her theological belief system. Thus religion inspires violence against other faiths due to the profoundly psychological need, based on the terror of death, for one's religion to be superior; and, because of the threat posed to the belief underlying one's own religion by other theologies.

Furthermore, the historical religions could not truly inspire happiness or fulfillment in the individual because they have been based on unproven and often wildly fictionalized stories or myths. Therefore, they can never adequately satisfy the inherent personal quest for truth and oneness with the universe and some God entity. Thus, religious belief has been and continues to be responsible for wasteful or violent behavior and war, both internally within a culture, and externally against other cultures, especially when those other cultures espouse a religious belief that conflicts with the myth underlying its religious belief.

(3). Summary: The General Failure of Religion in the Advancement of Humanity

Through religious belief, every human culture which has ever existed, offers its members with some, usually uniform and centralized, explanation for God and the Cosmos, as well as the promise of personal immortality, as a way to repress the death/meaninglessness anxiety. Religious faith is thus a form or method or cultural heroism enabling cultural members to establish a connection to the supernatural *Beyond* and to obtain a measure of self-esteem by following the mores and rules of the set down by religious dogma.

However, as made evident by the revolution in scientific knowledge over the past two hundred fifty years, individuals have come to suspect if not realize that the religious beliefs offered by the cultures in which they reside are based on false myth about the nature of universal and physical reality and thus misrepresent the true nature of God and the Cosmos. This revelation has caused many individuals to despair and hopeless longing because an essential component of the individual's LIE – the connection to a *Beyond* – that is, a God concept, and the promise of personal immortality in some definable afterlife, has been weakened if not entirely obliterated. Without that "immortality" component, the individual must compensate by focusing on other methods of heroism offered by his or her cultural group.

However, there remains a significant segment of humanity, due to a lack of education and the socialization process, which continue to adopt one of the ancient religious beliefs, such as Christianity or Islam, as a method to gain the needed personal self-esteem within the framework of religious dogma as well as the promise of personal immortality.

Religious belief based on false myth thus poses a three-prong problem for humanity:

1. It fails to resolve the individual's death predicament because past and present religious belief have inadequately and incorrectly conceptualized God, existence, and the afterlife;

2. Because no religion has developed an adequate or true conceptualization of God and the Cosmos, the existing false religions are left to war among themselves in order to assert that distinction; and,

3. The failure to adopt a genuine religion of mankind, which correctly envisions the God Concept, and the supernatural afterlife, has resulted in a jumble of religious belief that motivates ignorance and violence, and thus contributes to humanity's failure to achieve its highest potential as a sentient species.

The remainder of this chapter will explore both the underlying falsity of the myths of the major religions which have come to dominate and motivate the behavior of vast populations of humanity and review the record of such religions in terms of inspiring human beings to behave in such a manner as to enable the species to reach its highest spiritual, intellectual and technological potential.

(B). <u>The Failure of the Christian Myth</u>
(1). <u>Introduction</u>

There are approximately 2.1 billion adherents of the Christian faith in some form. While that number will increase over the next century, the Christian population in developed cultures have been declining over the past fifty years. This can be explained in some measure, by the rise of science and psychology which have both contrived to challenge the precepts underlying Christian myth and dogma – that is, the involvement of God in the lives of men, and the divinity of Jesus.

The central source of the Christian myth is, of course, the persona of Jesus Christ. Historical questions remain, however, not only as to the authentic details of his life, but as to the fact of his very existence. The versions of his life and works set forth in the New Testament and Gnostic Gospels have been attacked by historical and anthropological scholars as grossly inaccurate and unproven portrayal of his life. Indeed, the issue of Jesus' historical reality has been, and remains, subject of much controversy and heated debate, not so much in the popular mind as in the field of anthropological and historical study. Nevertheless, a consensus seems to have been reached among most serious scholars of the ancient Roman era that a person inspiring the rise of Christianity did, in fact, live in the period between around 4 B.C. to 29 AD, and that such person may have been crucified for crimes against the leading Jewish priests.

Whether Jesus existed and became a political figure, revolutionary zealot, Essene, preacher, prophet in the Judaist tradition, shaman, or visionary, and the meaning and veracity of the Gospels and remaining parts of the New Testament, is really beside the point and irrelevant to the suppositions underlying this Manifesto. The fact is that a myth and body of dogma, whether or not inspired by a real person, Jesus Christ, or the figment of someone's desire to establish a new religion (Paul of Tarsus, perhaps?) has evolved from a mythic figure we have come to know as Jesus Christ, and this myth and dogma has become known in its many guises as Christianity. It is the Christian myth which has been a controlling influence on the activities of countless *billions* of human beings for the past two thousand years and continues to influence the actions of up to approximately *two billion* people living today.

Indeed, irrespective of whether or not Jesus really existed, belief or faith in the Christian dogma he inspired remains a significant method offered by many cultures to its members for obtaining self-esteem, and for establishing a connection to immortality and God in the construction of the LIE for individuals residing in such cultures. This Manifesto unapologetically challenges the precepts underlying Christianity as false and, in some regards, ridiculous and puerile. Importantly, because it is a false myth, founded on an inaccurate cosmology, Christianity has failed, and will continue to fail, to alleviate the death/meaninglessness anxiety for its adherents; and, indeed, has inspired mankind to violent behavior and stunted intellectual and spiritual progress.

Moreover, because Christianity is based upon

false assumptions and myth, it must be rejected as a viable motivational force for any "genuine" cultural hero system proposed by this Manifesto. (This is not to say that certain of the moral teachings attributable to Jesus Christ, or inspired by his mythic existence, have no merit or place among the guiding principles in the new religion that must be a component of the Genuine Hero System proposed by this Manifesto).

The bold statement that Christianity is a mythical theology espousing a false cosmology, and that the "God" concept underlying its dogma is false as well, will, of course, offend many. But this Manifesto is not intended to mollify the masses or condone inauthentic human cultures. Rather, it seeks to raise mankind to a new level of spiritual and intellectual awareness in the hope of sparking true revolutionary change in the manner in which human culture is organized. To do so, the old methods of heroism offered by cultures, including the religious ones, must be debunked and dethroned in light of their abject failure to lift humanity to the highest level of thought and achievement.

(2). Fallacy of the Christian Myth

The essence of the Christian belief is that God became incarnate through Jesus Christ in order to reconcile mankind with Him, through Jesus' death and resurrection, after the fall from grace of Adam and Eve by their disobedience to His commandment not to taste the fruit from the tree of knowledge. That knowledge, of course, was death, and thus Jesus was sent to obliterate the terror caused by that knowledge. Jesus' death and resurrection brings salvation and the promise of eternal life to those who believe in him. Thus, Christians must accept that Jesus is God incarnate and that he defeated death by his resurrection.

Under Christian theology, as it evolved, the Jesus myth became a response to the story of Adam and Eve. Jesus was Christianity's antidote to Original Sin, the curse of God staining the souls of our ancestral parents, Adam and Eve, and their descendents, after they ate of the tree of wisdom and gained the terrible knowledge of their nudity (that they are creatures like all other animals) and of death. The Jesus myth tells us that God sent his Son to earth to save us from Original Sin – that is, to give us the key to overcoming death through Christ's resurrection. He died and rose again to show us that death is not the end and that, if we believe in Him and God, that there is no reason to fear death.

Christians believe that the substance of Jesus' teachings were recorded for posterity in the four "synoptic" Gospels of the New Testament – the Gospels of Matthew, Luke, John and Mark – which were written some years after Jesus' death, by most historical scholarship, between 70 and 100 AD. Those teachings underwent further evolution and inculcation until they formed a set or creed of complicated, and often, convoluted, disjointed and inconsistent rituals and beliefs.

After some three hundred years of incubation, the Christian dogma was ultimately summarized, as it then stood, in the Nicene Creed, first adopted in 325 by the then leaders of the Roman Catholic Church at what has been termed the First Ecumenical Council, or First Council of Nicaea. A second creed was adopted in 381.

A modern version of the Nicene Creed states the essential Christian beliefs as follows:

We believe in one God,
the Father, the Almighty,
maker of heaven and earth,

of all that is, seen and unseen.
We believe in one Lord, Jesus Christ,
the only Son of God,
eternally begotten of the Father,
God from God, Light from Light,
true God from true God,
begotten, not made,
of one Being with the Father;
through him all things were made.
For us and for our salvation
he came down from heaven,
was incarnate of the Holy Spirit and the Virgin Mary
and became truly human.
For our sake he was crucified under Pontius Pilate;
he suffered death and was buried.
On the third day he rose again
in accordance with the Scriptures;
he ascended into heaven
and is seated at the right hand of the Father.
He will come again in glory to judge the living and the dead,
and his kingdom will have no end.
We believe in the Holy Spirit, the Lord, the giver of life,
who proceeds from the Father and the Son,
who with the Father and the Son is worshiped and glorified,
who has spoken through the prophets.
We believe in one holy catholic and apostolic Church.
We acknowledge one baptism for the forgiveness of sins.
We look for the resurrection of the dead,
and the life of the world to come. Amen

The "clear and quite brief" essential message of Christianity is neatly summed up by Rodney Stark in his ambitious tome, *Discovering God: The Origins of the Great*

Religions and the Evolution of Belief:

> *Thus, Christians believe in an infinite, all-powerful Creator God....They also believe that God sent his son, Jesus Christ, into the world to atone for human sins through his death, thus providing everyone with the option to be saved – to enjoy eternal life. The Holy Ghost (or Holy Spirit) is the third "person" making up the Holy Trinity and is defined as a manifestation of God's abiding presence in the world, albeit all leading theologians have struggled to define Holy Ghost and many frankly refer to it as a mystery...As is evident, the principal doctrine is that of the Atonement, that Christ's death on the cross served as a sacrifice that reconciled humanity with God.*

But when the story of Jesus' birth, rise and mission is more closely examined, one is struck but it's unrealistic, fantastical nature, more a fairy tale than historical fact. Christians essentially believe that for some unexplained reason around two thousand years ago, God "decided" to become incarnate through the mechanism of "virgin birth," with Mary, wife of Joseph, a humble carpenter, as the female vessel by which his "Son" was to be conceived through the intervention of the "Holy Spirit." After incubating for nine months to term in Mary's bosom, God's son was then to be born in the most humble of surroundings. God "reasoned" apparently that the messianic prophecies of the Old Testament had to come to pass at that precise moment in history, so that a new covenant between Himself and humanity could come to pass and become expressed through his son, Jesus, and so that humanity could be provided with the means of conquering original sin imposed upon the species by the disobedience of Adam and Eve, the parents of the entire human species, when, at the behest of Satan, they ate the fruit of knowledge causing them to be cast from the

Garden of Eden. During Jesus' mission, he also provided humanity with the means to salvation and everlasting life in a Kingdom of Heaven that would come to pass after some future apocalyptic supernatural catastrophe that is bizarrely and cryptically described in the New Testament's "Book of Revelations."

For some unexplained reason, Jesus remained hidden from history and society for 30 years until he finally emerged from the unremarkable shadows to embark upon his messianic Mission of revealing the new God and new Covenant with humanity. Jesus' other message to humanity, in addition to the messianic, apocalyptical one, boiled the Ten Commandments of Moses to basically two: Love God, and love thy neighbor.

In any event, Christianity was founded on the purported teachings of Jesus Christ, God's supposed incarnation, although there is no contemporary evidence lending definitive support even for his existence. Indeed, some scholars have posited that he was created out of whole cloth as the prop for the new religion established by Paul of Tarsus – that is, St. Paul.

From these core beliefs, a complex code of rules and rituals (such questionable matters as forbidding the eating of meat on Fridays, changed later to only Fridays during Lent), the holy sacraments, and a vast political organization, have arisen. Over time, this vast organization of priests became the Holy Roman Catholic Church, a staunchly, hierarchical, autocratic and often-times militaristic empire extending its authority to many lands and sizable populations, and exercising substantial control over world politics and spiritual and intellectual discovery and pursuit. Indeed, the Catholic Church remains a complex hierarchy with substantial financial and political influence over world events.

In summary, the Christian religious myth can be boiled down to this: The God of the Old Testament used a human woman's body to birth his Son in human form, so that Son could die and thus absolve all human beings of the original sin of the first man and woman, Adam and Eve, and also to communicate a New Covenant between humanity and God which sets forth a revised code of moral and legal conduct by which men must live in order to gain salvation and immortal life.

Of course, there is no empirical proof for these claims. The Jesus myth remains exactly that – unproven myth. Indeed, there is no direct proof that Jesus even existed. The individual must accept the entirety of the Christian doctrine and dogma on pure Faith. Moreover, as will be seen below, that doctrine has motivated humans to cruelty and stunted the species advancement.

(3). Christianity As Inimical to Human Advancement

The consequence of Christianity's dominion over world politics and thought has been the stifling of the human spiritual, intellectual and technological advancement. This is primarily due to the fact that Christianity has compelled humans to believe a rather simplistic version of the nature of God and the Cosmos - that is, the myth that Jesus Christ was the Son-of-God, a God who directly cared and intervened in the affairs of mankind, and that salvation and immortality is attainable only by believing in the existence and role of Jesus Christ as the conqueror of the evil spawned by Satan in the final battle for the human soul in the Second Coming described in the New Testament Book of Revelations.

As demonstrated by the vast number of Christian believers, most of whom have been brainwashed through the socialization process into accepting its dogma and ritual as absolute and rigid truth, irrespective of their education, Christianity has flourished and come to be the dominant cosmological and motivating force influencing individual and collective behavior and attitudes in many human cultures. In these cultures, methods of self-esteem attainment are offered based upon the Christian dogma for fulfilling the individual's need to connect with a God concept and be assured of the promise of immortality.

However, with the onset of modernity and expansion of scientific knowledge, the essential underpinnings of the Christian belief as a viable explanation for the God entity and the cosmology of the universe has been seriously challenged. Thus, in the past century, the numbers of adherents actually practicing the Christian faith has markedly declined especially in developed cultures. Furthermore, the number of priests has alarmingly decreased causing the closure of many parishes and rumblings among the faithful that the Church should revoke its centuries old rule prohibiting priests from marrying, and even allowing women to enter the priesthood.

The shrinkage in the numbers of actual practicing Christians can be explained by the deficiency in the creed and myth underlying it as a viable belief for modern, educated humans. The premise of the Christian myth, in the face of modern scientific knowledge, has been demonstrated to be mere fantasy, borne, as Becker understood, by the stark need for human beings to find a system that alleviates the fear of death and consequent lack of the meaning of one's life which the prospect of death darkly inspires. The inviting answer to the human dilemma offered by Christianity via the promise of salvation and everlasting life through faith in the mythical figure of Jesus, son of the father-God, simply does not work anymore for millions who have abandoned the faith and who no longer socialize their children and others to accept the Christian belief as a viable avenue to self-esteem and the promise of personal immortality.

This Manifesto asserts that those who have turned away from the Christian myth have been right to do so. It is a false myth that cannot lead to human happiness or peace. No false myth ultimately is capable of providing relief from death and the unease of meaningless which death fosters in the human animal.

This Manifesto likewise urges all believing and/ or nominally practicing Christians to face up and admit the obvious – that their religious faith is based upon an unsupportable fiction, that it is a mere story, as believable and provable as the Santa Claus myth. Once that difficult task is accomplished, the leap into a genuine Faith in God can be attempted and realized.

(C). The Fallacy of the Islamic Faith

Islam is the second largest religion in the world, trailing only Christianity, with its faithful comprising approximately 20% of human population. However, Muslims (followers of Islam) are rising in significantly higher numbers than Christians. They are spread over vast areas of North Africa, the Middle East, South-Central Asia, and Indonesia. Indeed, although conceived in Saudi Arabia, non-Arab Muslims now out-number Arab Muslims by almost three-to-one.

As Christianity is the off-spring of the life and teachings of the mythic figure, Jesus Christ, the prophet, Mohammed (570 AD – 632 AD), is the source of Islamic faith. The story goes that in the year, 610, at age 40, while retreating into solitude into a cave in Mount Hira, Mohammed experienced visions in which he was visited by the Angel Gabriel. He subsequently received a series of mystical revelations. Although he initially doubted the sanctity and meaning of these visions, upon the urging of his wife, Mohammed eventually accepted them as revelations from God, and, as instructed by them, began preaching a message of strict monotheism. This message angered the leaders of his own tribe in Mecca, adherents of polytheism, and upon threat of death, Mohammed fled with his followers to what is now modern Medina, about 200 miles from Mecca.

Mohammed eventually succeeded in defeating the old tribes in several violent struggles, and he and his army took control of Mecca in 630. Upon entering the holy city, he destroyed the idols that had been worshipped there the past several hundred years. Within a year, Mohammed's army had unified all the tribes of the Arabian peninsula under the religion of Islam.

On June 8, 632, Mohammed died.

The two major, modern sects of Islam, the Sunnis and Shiites, are divided, with often violent consequences, as can be seen in present day Iraq, over the seemingly inconsequential and petty dispute as to who should serve as Caliph, the successor to Mohammed as the leader of Islam. Sunnis insisted that Mohammed's successor should be elected, while the Shiites demanded that the Caliph should come through the prophet's bloodline. The Sunni's prevailed, and now comprise 80% of the Muslim population. Of course, the early schism over the succession of the religion's prophet has evolved into wider differences in dogma and practice of the Islam faith between the Sunni and Shiite Muslims.

The major beliefs of Islam (which term itself means "submission" to the will of God, or Allah) are that God is one and that no partner is to be associated with Him (The sin of "ishrak" is to associate a partner with God; and, this idea makes Islam inimical to the concept of the Trinity espoused by Christians). Angels fill the gap between God and mankind and each person is assigned two - one to record good deeds, and the other, bad deeds. Muslims also believe that God has sent prophets to guide mankind from time to time, including Jesus, Moses, and others, but Mohammed is the only true prophet for all time. Indeed, Mohammed was given the holy book, the *Quran*, which among all holy books is the only one preserved in an uncorrupted state; and, God has decreed that a day will come when all will stand before him in judgment.

To summarize, Muslims believe that God revealed the *Quran* to Mohammed, who is God's final prophet. Mohammed is not perceived as the progenitor of a new religion; rather, he is the restorer of the original monotheistic faith of Adam, Abraham, and the prophets down the ages through Moses and Jesus, whose message had become corrupted over time.

The idea of submission to God or Allah, central to the Islamic faith, is obviously a clever psychological ploy enabling a person to avoid entirely the human awareness of death and resultant anxiety. The void of meaninglessness occasioned by the awareness of one's death, and consequent anxiety, is filled by one's submission to Allah. However, the Islamic method for filling the void should be easily recognized for exactly what it is – a rigid construct that acts as an intellectual, spiritual and psychological crutch against the crippling impact of the death/meaninglessness anxiety upon the lives of its human adherents.

That intelligent, rational and educated people – in this case, many millions of Muslims - having accepted as absolute truth the fantastical story that, in 610, God sent the Angel Gabriel down from Heaven to a cave in Mecca in order to restore faith in Him by incubating visions of the *Quran* in the mind of an otherwise ordinary Arabian tribesman named Mohammed, is understandable when analyzed under Becker's theory that death is the mainspring of all human activity, including religious faith, because of the human psychological need to repress the terror caused by its stark and frightening prospect. The extent to which the death/meaninglessness anxiety hounds humanity is amply demonstrated by the acceptance of such nonsensical and utterly farcical "truths" which form the basis of both Christianity and Islam, and explains why religions have become a primary and important method among many cultural groups as a means of overcoming the death/meaninglessness anxiety.

No doubt, the claim that Islam is a farce, a fiction developed over the centuries and accepted as truth based upon the human drive to connect to God and immortality as a way to repress or deny the death/meaninglessness anxiety, will be met by a chorus of perhaps violent condemnation from Muslims across the planet. Moreover, such likely rabid antipathetic response to the idea that religions, including Islam, are nothing more than fictionalized methods of death denial demonstrates the supreme difficulty of effectuating the drastic and revolutionary change espoused by this Manifesto in order to establish a truly just and progressive human culture. However, to capitulate to such attacks will be to risk the loss of the possibility sought by this Manifesto, which is no less than the survival of the species and a true understanding of the God concept and the Cosmos.

(D). The Failure of Other Religions and Sects

The other major religions of the world likewise

provide the members of the cultures in which they are offered a method for repressing the death/meaningless anxiety via a mythical explanation for God and existence that establishes an individual connection to a supernatural Beyond and the promise of personal immortality. As stated above, that is at bottom the purpose of religion, why it exists.

In addition to Christians and Muslims, other religious adherents number in the billions of human beings. According to a variety of sources, the following presents an approximate estimate of the numbers of members of various religious sects:

1. Secular/Nonreligious/Agnostic/Atheist –
   1.1 billion
2. Hinduism – 900 million
3. Chinese traditional – 394 million
4. Buddhism – 376 million
5. Primal-indigenous – 300 million
6. African Traditional & Diasporic – 100 million
7. Sikhism – 23 million
8. Juche – 19 million
9. Spiritism – 15 million
10. Judaism – 14 million
11. Baha'j – 7 million
12. Jainism – 4.2 million
13. Shinto – 4 million
14. Cao Dai – 4 million
15. Zoroastrianism – 2.6 million
16. Tenrikyo -2 million
17. Neo-Paganism – 1 million
18. Unitarism-Universalism – 800,000
19. Rastafarianism – 600,000
20. Scientology – 500,000

These religions and secular cults vary widely in their respective mythical explanations for God's relationship with mankind (or, as in the case of atheism, deny God's existence altogether), and what the individual must do to gain fulfillment and salvation. As noted above, the clash of ideas and explanations for God and existence among these religions, as well as Islam and Christianity, has caused, and continues to cause, great discord among human cultures often resulting in violence among their adherents and faithful.

(E). <u>Summary: The Stifling of Human Progress by Religion</u>

All religions, such as Christianity and Islam, are based upon mere stories, fictions, myth, which present inaccurate descriptions of natural reality, not unlike the mythologies of ancient times, or the Santa Claus myth, which have developed over time to give meaning to life in the face of death, and offer the promise of personal immortality. The dogmas underlying certain religions, such as Christianity and Islam, have gained a vast number of adherents through the socialization process because they offer a simplistic and readily understandable means of overcoming the death/ meaninglessness anxiety. Through fiction and myth handed down and massaged through the centuries, all the religions of mankind have succeeded in assisting their faithful in overcoming the fear of death by identifying a connection to a God concept, and by offering the promise of eternal salvation in some definable and mythological afterlife by adherence to usually simple and direct moral and mythological codes and laws.

Clearly, as demonstrated by the historical record, Islam, Christianity, and the other major and minor religions which have come to develop among cultural groups, have failed to facilitate the realization of mankind's spiritual, intellectual and technological potential. Indeed, they have largely stifled human progress by causing war for the sake of their respective beliefs, or for the sake of perpetuating their respective false myths about the nature of God and the Cosmos.

The result has been, for the most part, thousands of years of darkness and ignorance and contributed to the failure of the human species to attain its spiritual, intellectual and technological potential.

(F). The Role of Religion in a Genuine Hero System

This Manifesto calls upon humanity to forsake and abandon the ancient, mythical religions, which are out of touch with reality, and exchange them with a genuine quest for a comprehension of the true nature of God and the Cosmos. To do so, mankind must acknowledge two things – the existence of God, and the fact that at the present level of human understanding, we are unable to explain his genuine nature. Thus, the conclusion that religions have historically failed humanity in achieving its potential as a species does not mean that religious belief should have no role in the genuine hero system culture proposed by this Manifesto.

In short, this Manifesto does not ask, in the achievement of its purpose, that humans forsake religion or become atheists. Indeed, it is proposing just the opposite. Rather, it asks the faithful of all present religions to open their minds to the possibility that the myth and principles underlying their respective faiths do not comport with reality and do not satisfactorily describe the nature and purpose of God and the Cosmos.

Therefore, the role and experience of religious belief in the Genuine Hero System culture is based upon the recognition and strict admission that humanity, at its present level of spiritual and intellectual development and understanding, has not gained a true comprehension of God and the nature of the Cosmos, and all the attendant supernatural realizations which such comprehension may ultimately reveal. In the place of the myths underlying existing religious faith, the Genuine Hero System asks the faithful to embark upon a journey of discovery, a quest for the True God, the True Cosmos, and the true nature of immortality.

Such recognition of the failure of one's religion is supported by the fact that all religious precepts have been debunked by the fairly recent advances over the past two hundred fifty years in human scientific knowledge and general understanding of nature. Modern religions have thus been empirically invalidated as appropriate beliefs in any modern cultural hero system as a motivating force directing human behavior. The myths underlying Islam and Christianity are untenable with modern scientific understanding of reality and no amount of adjustment, redefinition or accommodation of thought, as has occurred especially in the past twenty-five year, will make such religious views compatible with what humanity through science has learned about the nature of reality, and to some small degree, about the nature of God.

A starting point of human understanding of reality was Darwin's evolutionary "theory" published in 1858. Based as it is on obvious empirical support in the physical, fossil record, in the field, and in the laboratory, there can be no doubt that human beings are the result of millions of years of the evolution of life starting from primitive and crude chemical smudge consisting of combinations of amino acids which, like viruses, came to mimic life, and eventually resulting, via the process of natural selection, in the multifarious, complex life forms culminating in the species, *homo sapiens sapiens*. Thus, except by resorting to the intellectual stretch of "Intelligent Design," the direct influence or connection of a caring and interested God in the creation of humanity (i.e., "creationism"), and then human affairs following mankind's creation, which underlies the Abrahamic religions of Christianity, Judaism, and Islam, has been finally and irrevocably debunked by evolution and other scientific discovery.

Likewise, the advances in scientific understanding of the Cosmos, starting with the theories of Kepler, Copernicus, and Galileo, that the earth and the planets revolve around a rather insignificant star we call the Sun in the far reaches of a rather ordinary and insignificant galaxy, and that we are not therefore the center of the Universe; followed by Newton's mathematical description of the physical workings of the Universe; to the enormous increase in the comprehension of the Cosmos in the 20th Century, based upon physical observation through advanced optical and radio telescopes, as an immense entity spanning vast eons; and, the complete re-working of Newton's understanding of the nature of the Universe, gravity and time, based upon Einstein's theories of general and special relativity and then later, quantum physics, have rendered the underpinnings of the Abrahamic religions obsolete, almost laughable.

In sum, especially in the last century, the foundations of Christianity, Islam and Judaism, and all other religious beliefs, have been swept away by a tidal wave of scientific knowledge and understanding; and, it is only by the stubborn refusal to accept the truth about the reality as demonstrated by the revolutionary scientifically based models, or through painful reformulations of their foundational principles coinciding with these scientific findings, do these religions remain viable beliefs within the hero systems offered by modern cultures.

This is not to say that the ancient religions are "dead," or prone to imminent extinction as viable beliefs offered by cultural hero systems to their members as methods of self-esteem creation in the bid to repress the reality and terror of death. Perhaps this is because the scientific movement, and its intellectual adherents, have failed to offer up an alternative to religious belief. In the process of condemning religion on the basis of scientific understanding of reality, scientists and intellectuals such as Richard Dawkins and his other atheist cohorts have ignored the basic human need to alleviate the death anxiety through adoption of some belief that provides a hope of personal everlasting salvation. Atheism, with its promise of oblivion, offers nothing except blank knowledge in present life, a life we know is subject to instantaneous and irrational obliteration. If some kind of God concept is not directly involved in the creation and existence of the universe, life is ultimately meaningless. Why live?

But humanity's recent accumulation of advanced understanding of reality does not mean that God has to be deemed nonexistent. Scientific understanding has merely redefined human understanding of reality. That does not mean that a God concept cannot fit within that reality. But fit it must to provide viable or genuine methods of self-esteem creation and the promise of personal immortality. Scientific understanding has debunked the description of God and His purpose offered by the main religions. It has not proven that God does not exist. Neither has science demonstrated that life is meaningless because of death; nor that the soul does not exist or that the individual does not live on in some afterlife. Indeed, as some have argued, the scientific theories for the evolution of mankind and the creation and physical essence of the Cosmos does not disprove the basic precepts of the old religions but only provides them with an alternative symbolic meaning.

In the face of modern scientific understanding of Nature and reality, humanity must become driven with the need to formulate a true vision of the God concept, that is, what God and the Cosmos and the immortality of the individual soul actually represent. That can only be done by first discarding old beliefs that no longer work toward an understanding of reality and God; and, second, by accepting a religious component of one's personal hero system – that is, one's LIE - that inspires one to a further and better spiritual understanding. That drives one to develop a genuine relationship with the true and actual God. In short, one must join in a collective human quest for a comprehension of God, and the soul.

The new religion of mankind must be based upon reality. Then humanity can accept a belief in some reachable *Beyond* which satisfies the urge to deny death, and gives real hope for salvation and immortality, not in some fake Heaven with angels and Jesus and the Prophets, but in a real afterlife based upon true spiritual, intellectual and scientific understanding. There will always be doubt in any religious system that will torment the human soul. But doubt should not be hidden, or made to be a sin; rather, it should be used to inspire the person, and the culture in which he or she resides, to keep striving endlessly, if need be, toward an understanding of the true God, the universe, existence, and the soul, in order to reconcile that doubt and perhaps, someday, to genuinely overcome it.

CHAPTER FIVE
THE FAILURE OF NON-RELIGIOUS HEROIC METHODS

History can then be looked at as a succession of immortality ideologies, or as a mixture of several of these ideologies.
- Ernest Becker

(A). Introduction: A Multitude of Empty and Unworthy Beliefs

To briefly recap, culture is, in essence, a vehicle for heroism – that is, it provides its members with the symbolic methods for the construction of illusory life projects, LIEs, which enable them to obscure or deny the reality of death and the meaninglessness of life and existence which such prospect implies.

A person's LIE, constructed from the available methods of heroism offered in one's culture, is fabricated by the individual through the process of socialization. A person's LIE imbues his or her life with meaning and purpose and thus gives him or her a sense of self-esteem. It is culled and developed from the aggregate set of methods for doing so offered by the culture in which he or she resides. One's life project is the product of one's inherited physical and mental attributes, together with indoctrination by family and social interaction during one's formative years. The LIE becomes a kind of shroud that inoculates the human wearer from the terror of death and meaninglessness. Indeed, being without such purpose – having no LIE, or having one's LIE rendered impotent, is the primary cause of depression and other mental illnesses.

One's LIE is the most important factor in directing or motivating one's behavior, and that only by its healthy and genuine development and advancement, can a human being attain happiness, fulfillment and mentally security. As this Manifesto has noted, the failings of mankind are directly attributable to the inability of past and present cultures to offer methods for the construction of meaningful LIEs which truly enable the individual to attain self-esteem and happiness in the repression of the death/meaninglessness anxiety while also collectively benefiting humanity. Stated another way, cultures have been unable to offer their members with the means to individual and collective fulfillment. Instead, they are offered trivial methods of heroism or methods that are inimical to the collective good.

Just as religious beliefs in every culture have failed to genuinely alleviate the death anxiety, or to do so in ways which fail to motivate humans to advance the individual and collective quality of life, as well enhance the survival of the human species, the various other non-religious methods offered by cultural hero systems fail to assist the individual in effectively repressing the death anxiety, and likewise motivate humans to destructive or inconsequential conduct. As Becker put it:

> *We have seen that what we call the human character is actually a lie about the nature of reality. The causa-sui project is a*

pretense that one is invulnerable because protected by the power of others and culture, that one is important in nature and can do something about the world. But in the back of the causa-sui project whispers the voice of possible truth: that human life may not be more than a meaningless interlude in a vicious drama of flesh and bones that we call evolution; that the Creator may not care anymore for the destiny of man or the self-perpetuation of individual men than He seems to have cared for the dinosaurs or the Tasmanians. The whisper is the same one that slips incongruously out of the Bible in the voice of Ecclesiastes: that all is vanity, vanity of vanities.

The following presents an overview of the various methods offered among past and present cultures to their members to enable them to overcome or obscure the death/meaninglessness anxiety. These methods are the motivational forces in human life, the forces that direct or inspire action and behavior. This Manifesto will explore each of these methods and identify why they fail to provide individuals with a genuine sense of purpose and self-esteem.

(B). The "Low" Heroism of Occupations

Becker insisted that human activity is essentially a response to the fear of death. Even actions related to what he termed "low" heroism, derived from the pursuit of ordinary or everyday occupations that serve the community in basic or necessary ways symbolically enables the person engaging in them to repress the death/meaninglessness anxiety. Thus, the baker and candle-stick maker can obtain a measure of relief from the terror of death by a job well-done in service of those who use his products. Of course, add to that mixture the symbolic pecking order and relational system among supervisor, subordinates, and employees, that is termed, "office politics," and another layer of false symbolic meaning is given to the occupations performed by humans. Moreover, the obsessive pursuit of "low" heroism explains the workaholic, the person who derives pleasure and meaning solely from his or her job.

All human groups are organized in such a way as to satisfy basic needs, such as gathering food, constructing shelters, and establishing protection from natural dangers, including other human groups, that enhances, if not ensures, individual and group survival. Human beings form social bonds precisely because by working together, they help each other in the mean and difficult activity of collective and individual survival.

Human cultures are organized so that their constituents are motivated to contribute to the general good of the group, thus insuring survival of the individual and the group. Employment in some capacity toward that general good, whether as a hunter-gatherer, farmer, warrior, priest, leader/organizer, mother, animal herder, factory worker, secretary, industrial scientist, CEO, lawyer, doctor, dentist, laborer, construction engineer, architect, contractor, roofer, factory worker, bank teller, real estate agents, etc., has become a method for attaining heroism in every human society because of the basic contribution of such activity to human survival and organizational advancement of the cultural group. Indeed, a central aspect of the family and group socialization process is to reward pursuits through education and occupation which directly benefits collective survival.

Thus, one's job in society fulfills the dual needs of enhancing the survival of the group while also becoming the symbolic means for constructing one's LIE. And for many humans, it becomes the main if not only aspect of one's

LIE, primarily because society requires that so much of one's time be spent in its performance.

Culture has thus ensured that doing one's job well is a means to self-esteem, and symbolically infuses one's life with meaning. Individuals are thus measured, and measure themselves, by the ability to contribute to the societal and general good in some fashion, by becoming and remaining gainfully employed in an occupation serving the society, and by advancing in the often complex political and social organization which arises from and in the course of that occupation. A job often defines the person, and therefore his or her self-esteem is often entirely dependent upon it.

That is why the loss of one's job through lay-off or retirement sometimes results in severe depression or even suicide. One's self-esteem, constructed from the job experience, is suddenly uprooted by the removal of that experience, and due to the time requirements of most occupations, the person is left without any remedial means by which to subsequently fill the void. He or she is lost, and no longer feels valuable. That feeling sometimes results in severe depression and grief.

Everyone recognizes to some relative degree that gaining self-esteem or basing one's LIE solely through occupational activity is not enough to bring satisfaction and happiness to one's life. Being the best baker in the world does not guarantee immortality. As in all things, death is the worm at the core, starkly informing each of us that the moment after one dies, another baker will be recognized as the best baker in the world. The needs of the group will dictate that a replacement be found. Though one's exploits, if superior, may be remembered and honored, the deceased will, in fact, hardly be missed. The memory of one's exploits will almost certainly dim over time if not become entirely forgotten.

This is the experience of everyday life. The death of one person, though tragic and sad, will not cause the extinction of the group or species, and each of us fully recognizes that ultimate and humbling fact. Individual death in fact hardly intrudes on the culture as a whole. Only spouses, parents, siblings and immediate family members are disturbed by the loss and sometimes even to them the grief is fleeting.

It is for this reason that most people find it necessary to combine the "low" heroism gained from one's job for obtaining one's self-esteem in the development of the individual LIE with other heroic methods offered by one's culture to overcome the terror of death. Those other methods almost certainly includes religion since, as discussed above, religion is the only method of heroic pursuit that adds the promise of personal immortality to one's life project.

While self-esteem through performance of one's job will remain a necessary component in a culture that embraces a Genuine Hero System, the individual will not be taught to rely solely on his or her occupation in the formation of one's life project to overcome the death/meaningless anxiety. Such a culture recognizes that its members cannot gain complete meaning from the performance of tasks necessary to the proper functioning and survival of the culture.

One's occupation in a Genuine Hero System culture will be given a different emphasis. In such cultures, most occupations will be designed either to obtain immediate survival needs for the group, such as through food production or construction projects, to increase the standard of living and life quality of others, such as through medical careers, or to enhance the eternal survivability of the human species through scientific research. Thus, in the Genuine Hero System culture, one's job is given the high purpose of attaining immortality for humanity as a whole, while benefiting all men in the immediate era of existence. While not enough to guarantee human contentment, it certainly will surpass the banal purposes of the occupational opportunities of current cultures that are based almost entirely on earthly benefits and narcissistic goals.

(C). Membership in Families, Tribes, Gangs, Cults, and Nations

Throughout history, identification with and exultation of social groups, however small in number, by their individual members has been a routine component in the construction of one's personal LIE. Members of families, tribes, gangs, athletic teams, fan clubs, social clubs, cult groups, and, of course, nations, acquire self-esteem through a prideful identification with and adoration of the entity to which such members belong as well as what that entity represents or to the ideals it espouses.

This sense of pride and belongingness is acquired through the socialization process. Our parents and schools provide us with a sense of community or national pride. Our peers provide us with a connection to each other in a basic friendships or in gangs which advocate various, and sometimes criminal, modes of behavior.

Members of definable groups form a strong bond and identify with other members, and firmly come to believe that the group to which they belong is superior to other groups, whether due to the physical appearance and prowess of its members, ancestry, artistic endeavor, or its ideas. It is that sense of superiority which vests them with the right to shun or mock members of other groups, or even, in the extreme though not uncommon form, justifies the commission of acts of violence and hatred or even genocide against outsiders in order to eradicate or gain dominion over them, and/or subsume them into their group. As noted previously, this prejudicial reaction, or ethnic cleansing as it is sometimes called, especially arises when the beliefs and methods for obtaining heroism through the construction of the LIE of a conflicting group challenges the precepts of the reacting group's beliefs for doing so, thus heightening the death/meaninglessness anxiety for members of both competing groups.

Group-worship thus furnishes a host of self-esteem enhancing methods for the individual through transference identification, kinship, patriotism, war, and prejudice. Such methods provide individual members of the group with an enhanced sense of purpose and self-esteem beyond merely performing an occupation which contributes to group survival in a more basic and direct way. Based upon a belief in the importance of the group, the individual is motivated to accomplishments which enhance its prestige or power and his or her position or recognition within the group. Of course, this often benefits individual and collective survival. Thus, one is willing to die for one's country in an otherwise senseless war because doing so provides the individual with a significant sense of self-worth and a kind of personal immortality via reverence by other members of the group. Gang turf wars in inner cities are a sub-set of this motivational force although recently such wars are also motivated by the materialistic urge to control the lucrative trade and dissemination of illegal drugs.

The ultimate expression of the concept of group-worship is nationalism. In <u>Imagined Communities: Reflections on the Origins and Spread of Nationalism</u> (1983), Benedict Anderson provided the following definition of nation:

> *In an anthropological spirit, then, I propose the following definition of the nation: it is an imagined political*

community - - and imagined as both inherently limited and sovereign.

In further defining the nation as an imagined political community, Anderson wrote:

Finally, it is imagined as a community, because, regardless of the actual inequality and exploitation that may prevail in each, the nation is always conceived as a deep, horizontal comradeship. Ultimately it is this fraternity that makes it possible, over the past two centuries, for so many millions of people, not so much to kill, as willingly to die for such limited imaginings.

Anderson traces the rise of nationalism to its cultural roots in religion, and specifically, at least in Western culture, to the decline of religious belief. Thus, he writes: "...in Western Europe the eighteenth century marks not only the dawn of the age of nationalism but the dusk of religious modes of thought." With the decline of religion as a means of obscuring fatality, Anderson proposed that "what was then required was a secular transformation of fatality into continuity, contingency into meaning...few things were (are) better suited to this end than the idea of nation. If nation-states are widely conceded to be 'new' and 'historical,' the nations to which they give political expression always loom out of the immemorial past, and, still more important, glide into a limitless future." Thus, Anderson saw one's loyalty and devotion to nation as replacing God as the individual's vehicle to self-esteem and personal immortality.

However, that construct may unduly simplify the equation representing the person's pursuit of self-esteem and immortality in the construction of his LIE overcoming the death/meaningless anxiety. Rather than being exclusive of religion, replacing it as a source of heroic relief from death, the devotion to the nation-state may merely have served to eclipse the religious method as the primary or sole source of such relief. For as Becker realized, devotion to nation is never enough to overcome the fear of death. Ironically, through the educational component of the socialization process giving rise to one's nationalistic fervor, the person comes to the realization that all nations are transitory, tangible, human concepts which themselves are doomed to eventual demise.

Thus, no matter the degree of one's patriotism and passion for his or her nation, he or she must also find some connection to supernatural existence through belief in some God in order to satisfy the urge to deny the reality of death. Indeed, most nations offer their citizens some mythical idea that it has gained the favor of God. In the United States of America this is no better illustrated by the motto on its currency and on many of its patriotic structures: "In God We Trust;" and, a source of rabid debate among its politicians concerns the need for God in the public discourse or in the justification of policy. In short, the mere passion for nation is, for most, never enough as the sole method for overcoming the death/meaningless anxiety.

With that said, nationalistic or group fervor and identification remains a key method for heroic pursuit in one's death denial project, and as has been historically documented, that passion partly explains the continuous tendency and willingness of nations and their leaders to go to war against other nations. Certainly, it cannot be disputed that nationalism, like religion, has led to vast destruction and the stifling of human accomplishment.

However, in a culture organized around the principal

of eternal human survival, the idea of separate nations is an anathema. Community identification in the genuine hero system can only be described as a wholly and completely human one. Only by the unification of human intellectual, spiritual and physical resources can mankind ever hope to attain a dignified standard of living for everyone, as well as the technological means to overcome the threat of extinction. To do that, human societies must reject nationalistic fervor as a motivating force, and replace it with esteem of the whole human community. The survival of the human species must become the group's underlying creed and individual self-esteem must be made to flow from that ideal. Becoming a person who contributes to the survival of humanity, in the short and long term, must be made an important means for gaining personal self-esteem. It must be a central method for the construction of one's LIE if mankind is to have any hope of avoiding the threat of manmade or natural extinction.

In short, in the genuine hero system, only passion for the "Human Nation" will be tolerated and be permitted as a vehicle to self-esteem.

(D). The Accumulation of Wealth and Consumerism As a Means to Heroism

Since humans first organized themselves into groups, and especially for civilizations that developed after the agricultural revolution, *capitalism* has been, and continues to be, the dominant economic and social organizing principal for such groups and civilizations. In capitalistic cultures, the means of production are for the most part privately owned and operated for profit, and the value of products and services are determined through the operation of the market-place system. Contemporary societies are predominately "mixed economies," combining both privately-owned and state-run enterprises for the production of goods and services, or mixing the characteristics of capitalistic market economies, and socialistic or communistic planned economies.

Whether a culture is purely organized under capitalistic or a mixture of capitalism and communist/socialist principles, money is used as a medium of exchange. Money is the legally accepted token or other object, usually currency or coin, produced by the government of the society, which is used for the payment or exchange of goods and services and in settlement of debts. Money serves as the standard of value for measuring the relative worth of various products and services and as a store of value. In short, in every human culture today, the accumulation of money is required to enable the individual, family, tribe, or group to obtain shelter, food, furnishings, and other necessities, as well as luxury or superfluous products and items which are not necessary for basic survival and sustenance.

The accumulation of money has become a basic and straightforward means of achieving self-esteem in the symbolic construction of one's LIE in the human pursuit of meaning. For one thing, the result of the amassing of money and wealth is essentially quantitative – that is, it is readily measured against such accumulation among other individuals across cultures. For another, the accumulation of wealth is universally recognized as a means to self-esteem. As Becker noted: "We disguise our struggle by piling up figures in a bank book to reflect our sense of heroic worth." The wealthiest among us are admired and envied, and become celebrities, sometimes on the bare accomplishment of their wealth whether it be earned or inherited or whether or not the moneyed celebrity has an talent independent of the possession of wealth. Who among us does not wish to be rich and who does not envy (or despise) those who are? As

Becker also noted: "... the reason money is so elusive to our understanding is that it is still sacred, still a magical object on which we rely for our own entrance into immortality."

Thus, all cultures today, even those that do not entirely embrace the capitalistic economic model, offer activities enabling their members to accumulate money. Indeed, cultures which have not done so in some form as a method of construction of the heroic lie in the denial of death have been doomed to extinction. The demise of communism as an organizing political and socio-economic principle is mainly due, according to Becker and others, to this very fact – that they did not offer the individual with a means to self-esteem through the private accumulation of money.

Indeed, in communist societies, the cult of money was deemed evil, to be shunned. Hence, this primary ingredient of self-esteem construction offered in most societies was unavailable in communist countries, such as the Soviet Union and the Republic of China, resulting in perpetually sick economies in those cultures with extensive black market economies, due to the very fact that the individual economic self-esteem was incapable of being satisfied under the communist model. Indeed, in those societies, robust black market or underground economies arose partly to satisfy the individual need for products and services unavailable due to bureaucratic incompetence, but also to enable the individual to accumulate money and the means to self-esteem. Thus, it was the failure to provide an avenue for economic self-esteem by the individual accumulation of money and wealth that doomed communism, and it explains why most communist and socialist countries today offer some degree of capitalism in order to remain a viable society. (See, *How Capitalism Saved America: The Untold Story of Our Country from the Pilgrims to the Present,* by Thomas DiLorenzo, which provides an in-depth discourse into the significant role played by the implementation of capitalistic principles in the survival of the early colonial settlements of Jamestown and Massachusetts, and how it is primarily responsible for the rise of the United States of America as the preeminent world power).

However, it is clear that wealth accumulation as a means to self-esteem is ultimately deficient in obscuring the reality of death, and alone is certainly incapable of providing the individual with a sense of genuine fulfillment and happiness. It is readily apparent to the individual that the illusion of self-esteem provided by the vehicle of money accumulation and, its offspring, consumerism or materialism, presents merely transitory, "here-and-now" gratification that is incapable of transcending death in any capacity beyond the earthly realm. A legion of wise quotes, not to mention human experience, and literary reference, are consistent in the admonishment that wealth alone does not deliver individual happiness or escape from death.

For example, Dickens' character, Ebenezer Scrooge, in his famous novel, <u>A Christmas Carol</u>, certainly found a measure of self-esteem in the accumulation of gold coins, but at the expense of his humanity and feelings of harmony with his fellow human beings. Indeed, recent economic writings have noted that the accumulation of riches above a certain level does not make citizens in wealthy countries any happier. Various studies have found that once a country has a per capita income of about $10,000 a year or more, the aggregate income-happiness link weakens. John Helliwell, in <u>Globalization and Well-Being,</u> (2002) argues that the curve flattens out at about half of current American per capita income, or roughly the standard of living in contemporary

Greece. These results lead economists to wonder whether a country's economic growth is important after all since increased riches do not equate to personal happiness, not to mention that the pursuit of money accumulation certainly does not enhance the quality of life for one's fellow man or enhance the survivability of the human species. And, as noted above, the pursuit of money as central to one's life illusion lacks any spiritual component, or promise of immortality. Hence, the proverb, "You can't take it with you," accurately reflects why the cult of money ultimately fails to provide human happiness.

While capitalism, of all socio-economic organizing ideas, has enabled certain societies to attain significant technological advancement and a marked enhancement of the quality of life and pursuit of happiness for certain of its members, it ultimately has failed to enable the species to fulfill its spiritual and intellectual (or even technological) potential. Moreover, individual members of capitalistic cultures seem no less tormented by the prospect and terror of death than their brethren in cultures organized under other economic systems. In short, wealth does not alone create a happy and secure individual because material wealth does not resolve the issue of death or explain the meaning of life.

Although money as a medium of exchange may initially continue being a tool of the species for fostering transactions of goods and service among individuals, in the hoped-for global Genuine Hero System human culture envisioned by this *Manifesto,* money will have a diminished role since the accumulation of wealth and rampant consumerism as a method of heroism will be contrary to the underlying beliefs of such culture in improving the quality of life for all its members, enhancing the survival of the species, and embarking on a continuous and perhaps never-ending quest for the nature of God and the Cosmos. Therefore, the accumulation of wealth and consumerism in the culture offering a Genuine Hero System for self-esteem and LIE construction, will have diminished meaning, if any, and will have become minimized as a motivating force for human behavior.

As noted in Part Three of this Manifesto, this is not to say that even in a culture evolving toward offering a genuine hero system for the construction of the LIEs of its constituents, that capitalism will not remain the organizing principle of the socio-economic system of that culture. Indeed, it may be desirable to continue to employ capitalism for the production and distribution of goods and services in the pursuit of uplifting the quality of life for all members of a culture as well as for those beyond its borders in light of its track record of producing advanced technological cultures. Human beings are competitive creatures by nature, and thus an economic system highlighting this natural tendency may be the only workable one.

As will be further detailed in the chapter dealing with actual implementation of the genuine hero system, the concept of federalism, as refined in the United States Constitution, among existing and future cultures, will be offered as an organizing principle for the establishment of a more centralized and influential world government, whose ultimate role will be to keep the peace among its member states, as well as fostering the establishment and evolution of Genuine Hero Systems in each. The use of federalism in the United States has permitted individual states to experiment with various forms of government and other initiatives that, if successful, have spread to other states. Thus, cultures will be free to employ different socio-economic as well as political models to organize its government and society - capitalism, socialism, communism, and any mixture of these theoretical and ideological organizing systems.

Lastly, the accumulation of money as a vehicle to self-esteem is not necessarily a bad thing so long as it motivates actions which advance the quality of life for all humans, and enhances the prospects of eternal human survival. Moreover, what constitutes increasing the quality of life should be given a liberal view, and includes engagement of the arts and athletic endeavor by a culture's members as a means to accumulate wealth. Nevertheless, in a culture whose actions are guided by a genuine hero system, those contributing most to life quality and survivability of the species by tangible action should be most rewarded. Thus, in a culture embracing the genuine hero system, scientists and doctors will be considered occupations more important and thus lucrative than those involving athletic or artistic/musical prowess, a phenomenon that is hardly the case in the present world with obvious disappointing consequences to the species.

(E). The Romantic Solution and Sex Addiction

Romantic love is yet another means to self-esteem offered among human cultures to their members for the repression of the death/meaninglessness anxiety and for also providing the individual with a connection to something beyond physical reality. Of course, the basic biological purpose of mating is procreation, the very real physical continuation of the species. That is the essential purpose of sex, and biology has devised a way to make the act physically pleasurable. So why does the urge to mate and procreate become much more than a mere biological function in the human psyche?

Ernest Becker explained it as the "romantic solution"

to the problem of the death/meaninglessness anxiety, the means by which humans satisfy our "urge to cosmic heroism" via "another person in the form of a love object." (Denial of Death, 160). The love object infuses the romantically smitten individual with self-worth in the subconscious quest for death denial. And, because it is a biologically driven necessity, as is obvious from our own individual experiences, the "romantic solution" is an extremely important one in the pantheon of symbolic methods for denying death offered among all cultures past and present. This is evidenced by the fact that devotion to the love object can cause one to lose interest in all other aspects of one's LIE; and, why rejection, separation, or loss of the love object causes humans such abject anguish and grief. As Becker stated:

> *What is it that we want when we elevate the love partner to the position of God? We want redemption – nothing less. We want to be rid of our faults, of our feeling of nothingness. We want to be justified, to know that our creation has not been in vain.*

Romantic love thus serves a similar function as religion, group identification and nationalism, and materialism, in assisting the individual to repress the death/meaningless anxiety. It takes on the aura of spiritual connection to something higher, much more significant than the self. Therefore, when the love object is lost, either through rejection or, more commonly, through the attrition over time of one's adoration, as Becker saw, because, after all, the love object is only human, the lover is forced to either seek a new love object, as is often the case, or find repression of the death/meaninglessness anxiety in some other method or methods offered in the cultural hero system for that purpose.

As Becker also saw, because the individual must come to the realization at some point in his or her psychic wanderings through life that the love object herself or himself is a mortal creature, doomed to die, the romantic solution is recognized, at bottom, as no solution at all. This acknowledgement renders the person helpless, and the loss suffered is equal to rejection by, or death of, the love object. Becker saw the abject dejection which such realization imposes on the individual. Or, as Jonathan Swift put it:

> *No wonder how I lost my Wits;*
> *Oh! Caelia, Caelia, Caelia shits.*

This starkly points out the absolute contradiction between the state of being in love and awareness that the beloved is a physical creature with excremental function who is doomed, like the lover, to die.

Every kind of violent, perverse, stupid and disgusting, or seemingly irrational or mad and unexplainable behavior on the part of human beings can be explained by a method or methods of heroism offered by a culture or based upon cultural. And the romantic solution to the problem of death is no different. Indeed, it often motivates some of the worst acts of violence and cruelty among the heroic methods offered by cultures for death denial.

For example, some years ago, in Buffalo, New York, a 49 year old man, the father of two, murdered a 22 year old co-worker out of jealously over the co-worker's internet relationship with the same 18 year old college freshman even though, as it turned out, the "freshman" was in actuality the girl's mother posing as her in an internet chat room that included the victim and murderer. What could possibly have motivated such a senseless act of murder?

While the murderer's attorney promised to appeal the twenty year sentence imposed on the his client based upon a claim that he suffered from diminished mental capacity due to internet addition, it can be argued that the murderer had constructed a LIE based upon his romantic "addiction" to his internet lover that was shattered by his discovery that she was carrying on a relationship with the eventual murder victim. This discovery and the consequent destruction of his life project – his LIE, left the murderer without purpose, starkly facing the meaningless of his life and the anxiety of death alone, without, sort of speak, the safety net of another heroic method. This set off a rage in his mind based upon the onslaught of anxiety occasioned by such loss of purpose that resulted in the inevitable destruction of his opponent by murder. Indeed, it appears he set up a parallel LIE to satisfy his sudden need for self-esteem which motivated him to an act of murder. The act of murder itself thus became another road to immortality and repression of the death meaninglessness anxiety.

This type of murderous and suicidal conduct is not uncommon among jilted lovers and it can be explained once it is understood and accepted that the LIE is a powerful motivating force directing all kinds of human behavior, good and bad. As an aside, one must conclude that the mother who was impersonating her daughter online was also driven by her need to repress the death/meaninglessness anxiety through that medium, albeit in a deceitful and perverse manner.

One must therefore recognize the daunting capacity for romantic love to enslave human purpose, especially because of its biological/instinctual nexus through the urge to procreation. This is not to suggest that human beings need become resistant to "falling in love." They merely must remain mindful of its enslaving capacity. The individual must be reminded, or remind himself of the gross power of love as a belief method in one's life project so that the pursuit of the love object does not detract from, to the level of psychological infirmity, the individual's pursuit of tasks, based upon other belief methods for attainment of self-esteem making up one's life project which more directly contribute to the general good and cosmic human survival. And it must be remembered that commitment to the love object serves the very real and direct purpose of sustaining the species through the procreation such commitment also engenders.

Thus, the Genuine Hero System proposed by this Manifesto does not eliminate romantic love from the pantheon of its belief methods offered to individuals for the attainment self-esteem and construction of one's LIE in the human quest to deny death. Human biology would thwart the attempt to do so in any event. Furthermore, romantic love can become a necessary component of the self-esteem project provided it is advanced by the individual with the restraint of will and intellectual and spiritual maturity that it merits.

The problem is that modern societies do not suggest such approach, and all too often romantic love runs amok, causing unhappiness and dissatisfaction in its wake due the failure of appreciation that the love object can never live up to the lover's expectation and should not be the sole source of esteem and LIE building. The love object is incapable of bestowing immortality, and this fact must be recognized by the individual from the inception of the relationship in order for that relationship to have any hope of surviving and sustaining itself in a truly meaningful and mature manner. The love object may only be a useful and complimentary aspect of one's LIE.

(F). The Glory of War

In his famous treatise, *On War* (1854), Karl Von Clausewitz wrote that war was "...an act of violence intended to compel our opponents to do our will." He also stated the famous maxim that war is "the continuation of policy by other means." While subsequent historians, philosophers or moralists may debate this claim (See, Robert Kagan, *A History of War,* 1994), there is no dispute that humans resort to organized, acceptable killing of other humans, known as warfare, in order to advance the economic, ideological, religious, and/or territorial interests of one cultural group against and over another.

Ironically, once it is engaged in by a culture, warfare serves the purpose of offering an ultimate road to heroism in the individual's attempt to resolve the death/meaninglessness anxiety. Indeed, in some societies, warfare itself may have been waged for that very purpose rather than to achieve some definable interest of the tribe or group. What better way to define heroism, to achieve the ultimate LIE, than on the battlefield, where, like the accumulation of money, the success or failure of one's actions in furtherance of the life project can be clearly and quantitatively measured by one's success at killing, and at avoiding being killed.

In his article, *The Glory of War*, Llewellyn H. Rockwell, Jr., made this point:

> But nationalism is not the only basis for bourgeois support for war. Long-time war correspondent Chris Hedges, in his great book War Is a Force that Gives Us Meaning *(First Anchor, 2003)* argues that war operates as a kind of canvas on which every member of the middle and working class can paint his or

her own picture. Whatever personal frustrations exist in your life, however powerless you feel, war works as a kind of narcotic. It provides a means for people to feel temporarily powerful and important, as if they are part of some big episode in history. War then becomes for people a kind of lurching attempt to taste immortality. War gives their lives meaning.

Thus, one can be a mere clerk one day, struggling to feel heroic in one's dismal LIE – stuck in "low" heroism, as Becker put it - and become a war hero the very next, winning the medal of honor for one's country and earning fame and praise among one's fellow cultural members.

The soldier involved in a military unit that is engaged in an operation of warfare is given a clearly defined set of beliefs around which he or she may realize self-esteem together with a connection to a kind of patriotic or group beyond, and a kind of personal nationalistic immortality. Staying in formation, obeying orders, the physical attack that is basic to the engagement of the enemy, are all avenues to the highest form of self-esteem in which successful endeavor is measured in life or death itself.

Throughout literature one can readily see the basis for war's allure. It is, at bottom, an escape from the banality of life, with the haunting prospect of death lurking in the antechambers of existence. As Philip Caputo noted in his memoir of the Vietnam War, *A Rumor of War:* "... I had one of those rare flashes of insight: the heroic experience I sought was war; war, the ordinary man's most convenient way of escaping from the ordinary."

Thus, one revels to escape into war because everyday heroism doesn't quite satisfy the human need to overcome the death/meaninglessness anxiety. Indeed, the death anxiety succeeds in overshadowing ordinary life, darkening everything we do and accomplish. War sells to the popular imagination not because it is a moral or just way for human groups to solve their problems, but precisely because it is another, concise and exciting means to solve the death/meaninglessness anxiety which confronts each human being every day of their existence. Moreover, it gives the individual a personal role and stake in the important and weighty, sometimes world-wide and world changing issues that are at the forefront of human experience.

Literary works are replete with passages and imagery glorifying the pursuit of war. Throughout Leo Tolstoy's epic, *War and Peace*, battle brings spiritual and metaphysical intensity into its characters lives. During combat scenes, soldiers are involved in intense experiences which heighten the sense of their own meaning in life. Men who were mediocrities and nonentities all their lives, like Captain Tushin, can function at heroic intensity during battle.

Indeed, warfare constitutes a kind of "genuine" or "actual" hero system without, of course, providing any constructive benefit toward the advancement or ultimate survival of mankind. The battlefield presents a theatre for the direct expression and true measure of heroism (kill or be killed) without the need for symbolic trappings. It is thus not unlike the sports arena, and hence the similar allure of both participatory sports and spectator-ism as methods for the alleviation of the death terror.

Warfare, of course, is starkly demonstrated to be antithetical to human advancement and will certainly become outlawed from the pantheon of methods to achieve heroic release from death offered by the Genuine Hero System. A society embracing the GHS will be driven by the belief in the sanctity and supreme importance of human life; and, therefore, the methods for achieving the realization of such belief offered for the construction of the individual LIE cannot include warfare as among such methods.

(G). The Vicarious Heroism of Spectator-ism

Everyday, millions of men and women attend sporting events, both amateur and professional, often spending a considerable amount per ticket, crowding into massive stadiums and arenas built at tremendous private and public cost, while others, usually parents, relative and friends of the participants, show up at sparsely attended fields or sports parks for youth or high school athletic contests. Millions more watch sports on television, listen on the radio, or follow the achievements of teams and players in local and national newspapers, magazines or on the internet. Spectator sports is gigantic business, with the spectators and fans spending billions on games and artifacts and all the accouterments, generating enormous profits for teams, sports venues, entertainment media, governments, and providing players at the professional level with substantial salaries and celebrity.

The attendance figures at sporting events are indeed staggering.   In both 2007 and 2008, the New York Yankees major league baseball team drew over 4 million fans. Worldwide, those individuals who attended amateur and professional games on every level certainly numbered in the high millions.

The phenomenon of "spectator-ism" is evident in every culture, no matter its developmental or technological level. In addition to sex and religion, interest in sporting events is an unwavering, similar characteristic among all human societies, no matter how great the differences in their economic, political, or religious belief systems. Indeed, there appears to be a basic need for cultures to offer its constituents with some form of "spectator-ism" in its panoply of methods for the alleviation of the death terror in their systems for heroic achievement.

In short, we human beings love religion, work, war, falling in love, sex, shopping, and sports, and not necessarily in that order.

Spectator-ism, as we portray it here, means the actions of an individual to become emotionally invested in the performance of a team and/or player and the outcome of a competitive athletic contest. The success or failure of the team and/or player is imputed to the individual. Moreover, that success has the capability of building self-esteem in the individual in his or her drive to overcome the death/ meaninglessness anxiety. This type of heroism is vicarious or virtual in the sense that it is not related to the individual's actual behavior, actions or participation in the event, but is dependent on the actions of others – in this case, athletes and teams – over which the individual "fan" has no control. (Participation in amateur sports contests – slow-pitch softball, bowling, golf, and others in local communities, is yet another form of heroic striving undertaken almost religiously by individuals which is yet another avenue to death denial).

The explanation for the vast and consistent appeal of spectator-ism among so many individuals is that it provides an ideally quantitative and easy vehicle for self-esteem creation in the urge to deny death and the meaninglessness of life. One gets lost in the achievement of one's favorite team and its players, providing a kind of vicarious or imputed thrill, because such achievement makes one forget, for the moment anyway, the stark reality of death. Indeed, the sports spectacle is a microcosm of life itself. If the team wins, or the athlete succeeds, a small measure of victory has been gained over defeat – or death.

By the psychological phenomenon known as *transference*, humans are able to assume the identity of the players and teams in their quest for victory and athletic accomplishment, representing, of course, the symbolic defeat of death and promise of immortality. "The thrill of victory and agony of defeat" are true emotional responses for the very reason that victory, even for the vicarious spectator, gives the sense, albeit momentary, of everlasting life, of immortality, while defeat reminds one of the futility of existence due to the inevitability of death. The word "fan," itself, the name given to a person who engages in athletic spectator-ism, is believed by some to be derived from fanatic, which means "a person marked or motivated by an extreme, unreasoning enthusiasm, as for a cause." What else explains the sometimes immediate wanton and destructive "celebration" by residents of those cities whose sports team have just won a championship in some major professional sport, or the gloom which descends upon the residents of those cities whose team lost the big game? Indeed, crime statistics consistently reveal that cases of domestic violence rise dramatically in those cities whose sports teams have lost the big game especially in the immediate aftermath of the event.

Ritual and minute attention to statistics and record-keeping is also symptomatic of sports spectator-ism, giving the activity a religious aura, quality and feel. Stadiums are often compared to cathedrals where the players and teams are worshipped like godlike and sacred icons. A whole terminology and dogma surrounds each sports, and hours are devoted in the broadcast media to discussing the relative merits of players or teams or the outcome of a specific contest.

In sum, the human obsession with spectator sports in its many guises - with the outcome of sporting events, and the performance and accomplishment of sports teams and their players - is motivated by the ever-present human urge to create illusions of meaning in order to repress the death/meaninglessness anxiety. Spectator sports is an ideal vehicle for satisfying this urge because of the decisive results of athletic contests, and the seeming everlasting prospect of the engagement of such events. Hence, the attendant fascination by most fans with seasonal and career statistics and off-season news.

However, as a result of modern culture's obsession with spectator sports with the rise of the communication media, especially television and the internet, other, more significant problems and needs of humanity are slighted or ignored and forgotten. The passion of millions of fans, and the financial commitment to athletic endeavor, could and should be redistributed toward activities which increase the quality of life for all humans, and which enhance the survivability and spirituality of the species. In short, the intellectual, spiritual, physical, and financial resources of the culture could be better spent on activities which inure to the individual and collective good, instead of being diverted to what are ultimately trivial, illusory and transitory pursuits in the human fascination with athletic contests.

The cause for the obsession with sports, together with its wasteful ends, is perhaps no better illustrated than by the donations of millions upon millions of dollars by college alumni to their alma maters in an effort to advance and enhance their respective intercollegiate sports programs. An especially troubling example of this waste was the donation in 2006 of $165 million by Oil tycoon, T. Boone Pickens, to his alma mater, Oklahoma State University, for the construction of a new football stadium and related athletic facilities. As reported by the Associated Press:

> *Pickens announced Tuesday he has donated $165 million to Oklahoma State to help create an athletic village north of the football stadium that already bears the name of the 77-year-old Texas oil tycoon. The money will go toward completing the upgrade of Boone Pickens Stadium and fund changes in a 20-year master plan yet to be approved by university regents.*

Mr. Pickens obviously derives a large measure of meaning in his life, and hence death denial, from the success of the OSU football program which, over the past years before his $165 million donation, had fallen on hard times. This is demonstrated by how bitterly Mr. Pickens takes defeat of the OSU football team, as he displayed during the HBO series, <u>Real Sports</u>, hosted by Bryant Gumble which aired on November 21, 2007 documenting his generous donation and devotion to OSU football. After watching OSU blow a 21 point lead only to lose on the final play of the game against the University of Texas, Mr. Pickens stormed out his corporate box, trophy wife at his elbow, barely able to restrain his disgust and disappointment with the last second defeat. Why should the loss of what was essentially a meaningless college football game have effected this billionaire so dramatically? Why do spectator sports, especially for fans at the professional and college level, have such similar effect, making one's life suddenly seem meaningless in the face of the defeat of one's sports team? As noted above, spectator sports are methods or vehicles for death denial offered by American and most other human societies, providing an opportunity for vicarious or imputed heroism, or meaning, through the exploits of the athletes and teams for whom the spectator cheers.

The success of the OSU football team, and the vicarious triumph stemming from it, constitutes an important part of oilman Pickens' Life Immortality Elusion or LIE. Of course, this is not the only method of heroic relief comprising Mr. Pickens' LIE. However, it is obviously important enough to have inspired him to donate millions of dollars to become an integral part of that method of heroic pursuit in his life.

Oil-man Pickens' investment further highlights the problem generally with modern human cultural hero systems, in that it demonstrates how trivial, or apparently meaningless activities, in terms of their slight or negligible contribution to the quality of individual life, or the collective good, are imbued which such importance in the death denial game. Mr. Pickens' monetary, spiritual and intellectual focus upon and dedication to the OSU football team may infuse his life with meaning. However, the success of OSU football in the grand scheme of things will have little, if any, impact or value to the improvement of the quality of individual human life; in no discernible way enhances the prospect of human survival; and, adds nothing to the intellectual, spiritual and technological advancement of humanity.

Stated another way, might not all that money have been better spent on activities directly related toward those ends? Under a genuine hero system, where the methods of heroic relief are designed toward improving life quality, enhancing human survivability, and generally advancing the spiritual, intellectual and technological potential of the human species in mind, the answer would surely be a resounding and definitive, Yes!

This does not mean that sports participation heroism

and its offspring, spectator-ism, will have no role in a culture offering its members with methods for death denial under a genuine hero system. Athletic prowess and accomplishment are basic to the human urge to self-preservation, and hence are biologically wired into the human mind. We compete because it helps us survive in the world. However, athletic endeavor must not be allowed to attain a higher place than is deserved among the methods offered by culture for construction of the individual's death denying LIE. And interest in sports activity, whether it be by participation or by spectator-ism, must not overshadow and detract from other methods of heroism offered by the culture which advance humanity toward its optimal spiritual, intellectual and technological potential.

(H). Other Vicarious, Addictive, and Perverse Methods of Death Denial

To summarize yet again the basic precepts of this Manifesto: humans engage in various activities and interests to repress the death/meaninglessness anxiety. In short, we do the things we do to create an illusion in order to obscure or hide the stark reality of eventual and inevitable death. These activities and interests stem from methods which have developed in human cultures to provide the symbolic means for death repression. These methods are known as "hero systems" – that is, the collective methods offered by cultures to enable their members to construct illusory life projects, or Life Immortality Elusions (LIEs), that infuse their lives with self-esteem and meaning satisfying the psychological need to repress the reality of death.

The methods used by members of the same cultural group for LIE construction are based upon the historical socio-economic, political, and religious beliefs which have come to be developed and adopted by them over the years since the group first became an identifiable culture. Cultural members obtain an understanding or comprehension of the availability of these methods to construct the LIE in the socialization process of family upbringing, public education, and other social communications. Mental illness and aberrant behavior are caused by an individual's inability to sufficiently repress the death/meaninglessness anxiety by obtaining self-esteem and a sense of meaning from the culture's hero system.

Thus, acknowledging that the human need for repression of the death terror through self-esteem methods offered by one's culture motivates human behavior provides the key to understanding all behavior, including perverse, compulsive, vicarious and addictive behavior.

For example, it is common (and "normal") in all human cultures for parents, often in a substantial way, to gain a vicarious or imputed measure of self-esteem through the accomplishments of their off-spring. The phrase, "living through one's child" exemplifies this type of heroism enabling the parent or parents to repress the death/meaningless anxiety through the achievements, success, and celebrity of their children. It also explains the dedication and fervor of "stage parents," who go to great financial and emotional lengths in advancing the potential professional career of a child prodigy.

This is perhaps epitomized by the role of Earl Woods in advancing the golf career of his son, Tiger Woods. This statement of the elder Woods' dedication and effect on Tiger's eventual considerable success is from his CNN. com obituary:

Earl Woods was widely acknowledged as being the driving

force behind his son's remarkable career. The former Green Beret was a talented sportsman in his own right, being the first black to play baseball in the Big Eight Conference when he attended Kansas State University. He had been a member of the U.S. Army's special forces unit for two tours of duty during the Vietnam War. But it was as the mentor of his prodigious son that he first gained international recognition. "I knew Tiger was special the day he was born," Woods said in a May 2000 interview with The Associated Press. From an early age Tiger lived up to his father's expectation as he evolved into the dominant player of his time -- the youngest player to win the career grand slam -- and one of the most celebrated athletes in the world. PGA Tour commissioner Tim Finchem said Earl Woods will be remembered for providing Tiger every opportunity "to become the world's best golfer and an outstanding representative of the game and its values."

This begs the question why Earl Woods, as well as the many other parents who have pushed the careers of their children to ultimate success, devoted so much time and energy to furthering the careers of their respective prodigious children. Becker would argue that in the process of doing so, these parents derive a sense of self-esteem about themselves, and hence are able to achieve a means to deny death through the advancements of their children's career and hoped-for eventual success and celebrity. That is why parents whose LIE is dominated by this method of heroism become so bitterly disappointed, and even hostile toward their children, as well as his or her competitors, and those involved in the competitive process, when such success and celebrity is not achieved. Hence, the parental fights at youth sports events that is reported at regular intervals.

Other non-biological addictions may also be attributed to, or result from, the need of individuals to pursue heroic relief from the death terror through the obsessive performance of a certain activity. For example, addiction to gambling is not the result of a biological or physiological maladjustment, but rather stems from the individual's drive for creating and entering an illusion that denies the reality of death via the quantitative achievement of success, or thrill of undertaking risk, through the placing of wagers on various games of chance or betting on horse races or sporting events.

Likewise, while sexual pursuit is driven by biological need, addiction to sexual experience may be attributable to the human psychological need to obscure death. What better way to do that than to become lost in sexual pleasure through fantasy or actual engagement in such activities? How else can one explain the pervasiveness of pornography, and the perverse attention given to sex in the broadcast, print and internet media.

Almost every human activity, in fact, that is not related directly to survival, and even those that are through symbolic overlay, can be traced back to the human need to create symbolic illusions of meaning in an attempt to run from death, or to deny it, as Becker so aptly described the psychological phenomenon. Getting tattoos, becoming enamored with a musical style, and the attendance at rock concerts, becoming immersed in movies or television programs, fascination with celebrity – each of these is merely another of the many methods offered by human cultures to their members to obscure the stark reality of death by the illusion of meaning and importance which these activities are given by the individual, when, in truth, in the end, each of them mean nothing. They provide only an illusory escape. The problem, of course, is that the activities motivated by these "addictions," like almost all other human heroic pursuits, cause human beings to waste time, money and emotional and intellectual energy in activities that are trivial and do little to advance individual and collective well-being and growth.

Chapter Six
The American Hero

Each script is somewhat unique,
each culture has a different hero system.

...man's groping for meaning stems from the most
idiosyncratic individual needs. This is another way of saying
that each individual derives his feeling of self-value in a way that
is bound to be a little different form that of all others.
- Ernest Becker

In this chapter, the methods offered to persons residing in the United States of America – that is, the American cultural hero system - for the construction of their illusory life immortality projects or elusions – their LIEs - which assist them in repressing the death terror will be examined. Later in the chapter, a specific example of the LIE of an imaginary, ordinary American "Joe" will be detailed.

This Manifesto will argue that the American cultural hero system, likes its contemporaries, fails to foster, and in many respects is contrary to, the advancement of humanity to its highest spiritual, intellectual and technological potential and development; and, that it fails to generate a genuine sense of self-esteem in the individual but rather provokes unhappiness and discontentment.

America offers a wide assortment of methods based upon multifarious and sometimes conflicting beliefs for its members to construct their LIEs. America is not a single homogeneous culture but rather consists of sub-cultures each of which offers methods of heroism from among those that were detailed in Chapter Two. As Becker stated in the epigraph to this Chapter, each of us constructs a different illusion for death denial dependent on our origin of birth, our upbringing, education, and many other variables, including biological ones. For example, a person growing up in south Los Angeles will have a different set of methods of heroism than the person residing in Scarsdale, New York. Yet, as we saw in Chapter Two, there are certain general means or categories for constructing the life illusion in the quest to overcome death through heroism that are similar across even vastly different socio-economic cultures which have arisen in the United States.

The following presents a non-exhaustive summary of the various categories of methods for death repression available to the members of American cultural groupings:

1. Economic Method: The Accumulation of Money and Things

America has adopted a mixed form of capitalism and socialism as its socio-economic organizing principle. Self-esteem is achieved under this system by the accumulation of wealth via some kind of legal or illegal profitable enterprise or through one's employment. The more money one has, the more and better things he or she can buy, which leads to a clear-cut, quantitative measure of status and even celebrity among members of the culture. Under a capitalistic system, individual worth and class status are measures based upon materialistic values. That is, a person's value and worth in society is usually determined by the amount of money in his wallet or bank account, the size of his home, the kind of car he drives, etc.

Although capitalism as an economic organizing system is responsible for significant scientific and technological advances, it also motivates trivial or base behavior such as the pursuit of money for its own sake, and crass consumerism which are inimical to the genuine attainment of mankind's spiritual, intellectual and technological potential.

Indeed, advanced education is largely deemed a step in the ladder of success rather than the means to the pursuit of knowledge to advance one's intellectual and spiritual well-being. Success in large measure is defined by the attainment of a high-paying job after obtaining a college degree in order to obtain more and better consumer goods rather than a grand and altruistic quest on the part of the individual for increasing one's knowledge and understanding of the human condition in order to help humanity in its perilous journey through space and time on planet Earth.

Thus, via the socialization process, as especially evident in mass media, rampant commercialism and consumerism marks every facet of American life. Art, literature, occupation and athletic competition has become purely a quest for money, rather than the pursuit of knowledge, understanding and genuine happiness and fulfillment. That such happiness and fulfillment are rarely obtained by a person solely driven by his or her LIE to accumulate money and things is stark testament to the lurking power of the reality of death, "the worm at the core," as William James would say, to render a lie to that illusion as the foundation and motivating force of one's life.

2. Romantic Method: Love and Sex Addiction

Americans rely on physical attraction and emotional feelings of romantic love to find their mates, rather than on the mutual arrangements of families based upon class and religious belief. The love object becomes a source of fulfillment and self-esteem for the individual.

Hence, American mass television, radio and print media, and advertising concentrate on beauty, sex, and romantic sentimentalism and sensationalism in providing entertainment programming, and hawking products. Such programs and broadcast commercials widely appeal to the masses precisely because they cater to the belief that one's self-esteem is reliant upon such romantic and sensual attributes.

While some individuals rely on a romantic love object solely to satisfy their need for self-esteem in repressing the death terror, others use the physical act of sex or fetishism as a kind of opiate to do so.

3. Family Methods: Relationships and Pecking Order of Family Units

Death repressing self-esteem is also garnered by American cultural members through a strong affinity for family relationships and activities. The loss of that connection, either through dislocation or loss of loved ones through death often creates a serious emotional void and depression.

Complex and dynamic emotional ties are created

within extended and nuclear family units from which a person derives his sense of place and worth in a society. (Not to mention the central role played by the family in the socialization process for establishing the individual's adoption of the culture's hero system).

In addition, parents, especially in modern America, gain a measure of self-esteem through the exploits and successes of their children. The claim "living through one's children" is a very real and active component in the American hero system, and accounts for "stage" parents in all kinds of leisure, artistic, modeling, and sports endeavors who go to great lengths in an effort to assist their child succeed and excel in a particular activity.

4. Sports Related Methods: Athletic Competition and Spectator-ism

Due to America's great financial wealth, its members are afforded substantial leisure time in which to pursue death repressing, self-esteem enhancing activities. Most Americans spend that time in amateur athletic endeavors, such a fast-pitch and slow-pitch softball, golf, bowling, biking, hiking, skiing, running, walking, dancing, roller hockey, sky-diving, snowboarding, among many other athletic pursuits, through which a measure of self-esteem, through team or self competitive experience is gained.

In addition, Americans are consumed with watching professional, college and even amateur athletic and car racing events from which they gain vicarious self-esteem in the pursuit of heroic competition and achievement of the participating athletes that assists the spectators in creating an illusion that represses the death/meaninglessness anxiety.

The huge popularity of the major league sports

leagues such as the National Football League, Major League Baseball, the National Basketball Association, and National Hockey League, and other events such as NASCAR, the PGA, the PBA, where millions either attend the events, or watch or listen to them on television, radio or internet, respectively, is testament to the obvious fact that Americans consume and are consumed by these spectator activities. Americans are obsessed with their sports teams, favorite players, and events, spending billions of dollars on them, and many hours of their leisure time, and the reason for the obsession is that it is a convenient and ready means to death denial.

5. Artistic Methods: Painting, Writing, Singing, Composing, etc.

America offers a wide range of opportunities to its constituents for the pursuit of creative endeavors as avenues to self-esteem, from the literary, stage, television, radio and film, music, and classical arts.

As in sports heroism, Americans spend billions of dollars and many of their leisure hours attending or following musical and other artistic events. Again, the reason is that such pre-occupation provides the individual with a convenient escape from the prospect of death.

6. Religious Methods: Christianity, Islam, and others

The United States Constitution permits freedom of expression and thus a wide variety of religious beliefs and practices have been established in America although it is largely a Christian nation. Still, all the major religions exist and flourish, as well as fringe or radical denominations of these religions, together with a wide array of cult, metaphysical, and quasi-religious, New Age and various radical groups including Satanism and Wicca. Of course, atheism is also tolerated.

Each American religion, whether mainstream, radical, or cult, promises a direct connection to God, or provides some explanation for existence and death, which of course supplies the non-atheistic believer with the assurance that life and the existence of the Cosmos are purposeful (even though, as reviewed earlier in this Manifesto, the basis of such assurance or faith is often superstition and myth without any scientific or intellectual basis or confirmation of the underlying dogma supporting such faith). Most American religions also offer the promise of personal immortality through some kind of defined or coherent afterlife.

7. Nationalism or Group Identification

Not unlike persons residing in other nations around the world, Americans are for the most part extremely nationalistic and patriotic. Most espouse the national purpose, and identify with the symbolic and ritualistic representations of the country, such as flag, anthem, and military uniform. Such national spirit and love of country is primarily derived in each American from the socialization process. Americans identify themselves as such, and honor the country, because they are taught to do so by family, school, and media.

For the majority of Americans, being a member of the military and going to war is thus deemed a supreme and honorable form of heroic effort. Indeed, cheering for one's nation (e.g. the ever present chant at Olympic events, "USA, USA"), and defending it against interlopers, real or imagined, is similar in many respects to spectator-ism, where one identifies and garners self-esteem and a connection to something greater by rooting for the sports teams of a particular city, usually the one in which the person resides. (Hence, it is often foolhardy and dangerous for a person to attend an away game donning the symbolic uniform jersey of one's opposition home team). Thus, there can be no higher fulfillment of self-esteem than to actually defend one's country by joining the military and going to war.

The nation and national good thus become the vehicle through which the individual creates the illusion of importance, meaning and transcendence over death. One lives on through the nation, although there is an inherent recognition, deep down, that no nation lasts forever.

However, group identification and worship as a form of heroism is not limited to an expression and feeling of patriotic love of America. Americans feel such connections to smaller groups such as social and ethnic clubs, college fraternities, professional associations, sports clubs, and inner city gangs. Affiliation with and support of these national sub-groups is driven by the same need to become accepted and gain a sense of illusory belongingness one gains from identifying with the nation in which one lives.

8. Ideological Methods: The Cult of Causes

Starting or joining causes for some perceived social or national or local political good, such as feminism, environmentalism, property tax relief, etc., are activities engaged in by Americans which likewise provide an illusion of meaning and importance that overcome the stark reality of death.

As indicated above, the above-described heroic methods do not comprise an exhaustive list, but merely indicate a sampling of such methods available to Americans for construction of illusory life immortality projects infusing their lives with importance and meaning and thus enabling them to repress or deny the reality of death.

Let us now describe the life immortality project or elusion, the LIE, of a typical American "Joe."

Joe is in his mid-thirties, and is vice-president of a financial advice and investment firm with numerous clients and investors. He has been employed at the firm for almost ten years, and seems to have figured out and managed its political and social procedures that could eventually result in his promotion to senior vice president, and hopefully, partner with an ownership stake in the firm's profits.

Joe takes pride in his work, spending much time in research and study for the benefit of his clients, and is driven to maintain a level of excellence in his performance as an example to his colleagues and subordinates at the firm, and to win recognition and favor from his superiors.

A couple years back, Joe was transferred into a department with a supervisor who simply did not seem to like him, or acknowledge his abilities. He chastised Joe at every turn, and gave him a sub-par performance evaluation. Joe's sense of self-worth was markedly diminished by this treatment, and every aspect of his life, including his health and relationships, suffered for it. This supervisor eventually left the firm, and his replacement again recognized and rewarded Joe's drive and talents. Joe's performance evaluations improved and he was given tasks requiring more responsibility and ingenuity. Once he regained his confidence and measure of self-worth, Joe excelled in accomplishing the projects assigned to him, and with gaining new clients for the firm, and generally succeeding beyond expectations, earning him even greater praise and reward on his way, at last, to achieving his present, important status in the firm.

Joe spends between 50-60 hours at the office, performing his duties, and nurturing his political and social contacts at the firm in his quest to become senior vice president and, ultimately, full partner.

Joe fell in love with his wife, Sarah, while attending college. Although he has strayed into affairs twice since they were married thirteen years ago, he remains romantically and emotionally connected to Sarah. Two years ago, when she discovered his last affair, with a secretary named, Lois, her threats of leaving Joe rendered him heartsick and unable to do anything except attempt to resurrect their relationship which, after some weeks, he succeeded in accomplishing. Since then, he has resolved to remind himself of his romantic connection and need for Sarah in his life, and thus has not strayed from the marriage – except by meeting escorts from time to time to feed his sexual urges.

Joe and Sarah have two children, Gabe, aged twelve, and Marian, aged eight. Both are extremely intelligent and athletic. Gabe is an superior baseball player and competes on the little league team which Joe coaches during the summer months. Joe dreams that one day Gabe will play college baseball and perhaps even in the major leagues. Marian plays violin, attending various competitions, is a first class speller, and competes in school and county spelling bees. She is coached and nurtured primarily by Sarah.

Joe is an excellent tennis player and competes in various competitions. He has also become a long-distance runner and sometimes travels to compete in marathons.

Joe also has taught himself to play guitar, and spends long evenings perfecting his talent and writing songs.

Joe and Sarah belong to a local Catholic Church, and though not avid practitioners, do regularly attend. Joe has found the time to read scripture and has come to accept, through upbringing and faith, that Jesus Christ is the Son of God and the teachings of the Christian Church in which he and Sarah are members offer correct representations of the spiritual nature of life. He makes no effort, however, to reconcile the findings of modern science with the dogma of the Church.

Now let us imagine, like Dashiel Hammett's imaginary character, "Flitcraft," in *The Maltese Falcon*, some chance event, like a car accident or sudden illness, that almost kills Joe; and, during the time Joe spends recuperating in the hospital, he realizes that the construct of his life immortality elusion - his job, his romantic connection to Sarah, the exploits and successes of his children, his athletic prowess and victories in tennis tournaments and marathons, and his unpublished songs, mean absolutely nothing in the face of death. His life is a mere illusion, built on these methods for obtaining meaning in his life, which ultimately serve no purpose in the grand scheme of the universal experience. Once he is dead and gone, even if he lives to be one-hundred, in a thousand years, no one will have remembered him. Like his body, the illusion of his life would be mere dust. As forgotten and meaningless as if he had never lived at all.

Even his faith in the Christian God and Jesus Christ does not mollify Joe, because, during his stay in the hospital and all the time that gave him to think things over, he recognized that the Christian body of dogma. like all historic and contemporary religions, is a convenient construct as well, devised to make him and those like him believe that there exists something beyond this physical world. However, there is no discernable proof of that afterlife offered by Catholicism except faith. Such inspiration of such faith is nothing more than a form of brainwashing by the religious fathers and priests, who, of course, have much to gain by obtaining and maintaining believers in that faith. If people cease to believe, they will be out of work. But even worse than that, the loss of faith by others diminishes their own faith and illusion that they are representatives of Jesus and God in the physical realm.

Joe naturally falls into a deep depression from the experience, from which he will eventually emerge once he returns to the world and his time of reflection is curtailed by interaction with others and the return to activities and employment. His life/immortality elusion will be re-built, like his body, but now with the same doubt that maturity and aging and the recognition of one's mortality brings to those who enter into the final stage of life known as old age or senility.

Then comes along other methods available for constructing one's self-esteem, based upon the belief in the human species as a sacred part of the universe, and the sanctity of the life of each and every human being. These methods require that humans perform activities that enhance the quality of life for other humans, and/or which enhance the survivability of the species into the distant eons.

The new Joe decides that attempting to reconstruct his life immortality project from the existing methods available to him in the American cultural hero system will never make him content and happy because of what was revealed to him during his recuperation from his near-death experience. He quits the investment firm, and returns to school to learn a trade that will enable him to benefit his fellow man. He joins a group that is spreading the word of rejection of false heroism. He has become a member, a happy and contented member, of the new culture of the genuine hero system.

His new illusion is no longer really an illusion at all, but a recognition that death is the only reality, the only motivating force in his life. He begins a new life in service of his fellow man, and of the human species, and embarks upon a quest to understand the true nature of God and the universe in which he lives. He is happy, at long last, because he is no longer leads a false , automatic life, but a authentic one, based upon reality.

This American "Joe" has finally joined the sacred family of the humanity

Chapter Seven
An Aside: A Theory of Reality and Illusion

Cogito, ergo sum
- Rene Descartes

(A). <u>The Concept of Reality</u>

What is real, and what is illusion?

This question has haunted mankind since the dawn of time. It continues to haunt us as evidenced by the numerous books which have been published in recent years which question our comprehension of reality in light of scientific discoveries in quantum physics and regarding the nature of consciousness itself. (See, *Busting Loose From the Money Game,* Robert Scheinfeld, as well as the enormously popular *The Secret* and cottage industry of tapes and DVDs that have developed from the "law of attraction" it espouses which is merely a restatement of the concept by William Wattles, Napoleon Hill, and others writing in the early and mid-1900s).

Five hundred years ago, Descartes speculated that the only reality we can be sure of is that we exist; and, that we know of the reality of our existence simply because we are able to think about it. To put it as he famously did five centuries ago:

Cogito, ergo sum!
"I think, therefore I am!"

Of course, our ability to think, and acknowledge our existence, concomitantly provides us with the awful awareness of the converse - our eventual non-existence through the physical mechanism of death. Thus, because we think, we can satisfy ourselves that we exist – that we are, and also that some day, we will not exist, that is, that we are not. Stated another way, the ability to think has enabled each of us to become terribly aware not only of ourselves and surroundings, but that, at some unknown date and time in the not-so-distant future, our physical bodies will decay and die and turn to dust. With death, the ability of our brains to generate the electrical energy considered to be "thought" will cease.

Thus, we can be sure of not one, but two realities – that because we think, because by some physical property, we generate the necessary electrical energy comprising thought, we are; and, that someday, we are not. Beyond that, nothing else is real. Absolutely nothing. Nothing we do in our lives has meaning outside and beyond that pure perception and acceptance of reality.

Symbolic trappings may be, and have been, constructed around these essential and obvious truths in order to infuse life with meaning, and to provide an individual or group of individuals with an illusory basis for motivating action; however, at bottom, there is no reason to act at all, except of course to satisfy the individual's biological, self-preserving urge to eat and procreate, defecate in order to survive both individually and to contribute to the species' survival through the exchange of our sexual fluids. We must eat to survive, therefore food must be gathered; and, a group of humans, familial in origin, of course, spreading out into a confederation of family units, must be organized in such a way as to foster the gathering of food, construction of shelter, and defend food, shelter, and themselves from human and non-human predators. The social group must also be organized in such a way as to facilitate breeding in an orderly and efficient manner. The group must be replenished, so the biological urge to procreation is imperative.

However, while the activities of assisting in the survival of oneself, and the group, may give actual and symbolic meaning to the life of the individual, and vest him or her with a form of "low" heroic self-esteem (for being a worthy food gatherer, or shelter maker, or protector from predators), as we have seen, gaining one's self-esteem through these efforts is simply not enough to alleviate the terror and anxiety caused by the acknowledgement and awareness of the dual realities of existence and death especially when the culture develops enough to provide leisure time to its members to consider the human condition. No matter what one does in the earthly realm to gain self-esteem, the reality problem always becomes evident and death, the worm at the core, reveals itself.

Thus, the individual is driven to adopt a belief or faith in some higher or cosmic purpose, some illusion, offering the promise of personal importance and meaning, not to mention, immortality in some supernatural afterlife, to escape from the realities of existence and death. (Indeed,

Becker and others have surmised that it is the biological urge to basic survival which may spawn the individual's quest for eternal existence; and, this urge gives impetus to the person's desire to symbolically and ritually adopt a belief in the possibility of eternal life by imagining a God concept and a related dogma answering this quest for divine immortality).

As demonstrated by history, human understanding of the nature of the physical universe has increased, evolving over the slow advance of years and eons to a more complete comprehension of the actual nature of existence and the universe. Human hunter-gatherer groups had a different conception of reality than those humans who obtained their sustenance through agricultural pursuit. Indeed, with the invention of agriculture, complex organizations of mankind were able to form and develop into vast, multifarious civilizations. This provided certain individuals within the civilization with sufficient leisure time to more fully consider the nature of reality, to think about existence and death, and come up with explanations for both in order to deliver the promise of eternal salvation to satisfy the basic and inherent human biological and psychological will to survive. The ideas and constructs for reality, which ultimately became settled religious dogma in the earliest civilizations, were based upon a particular understanding of the nature of the universe that eventually arose in the civilization and became accepted as truth.

Thus, the first human civilizations, with little comprehension as to the actual nature of the physical world and natural universe, still found it necessary, of course, to postulate creation myths and other cosmological explanations for the presence of humanity on earth, and for the very existence of the physical world. These explanations were invariably incorrect, and as mankind attained more knowledge and understanding of the natural world, and/ or his ideas about the nature of God changed, new and different cosmological realities imposed themselves upon human cultures. The result is the modern culture, a mixture of superstitious and scientific understanding that sometimes manage to co-exist in uneasy alliance in the minds of men.

Primitive and ancient cultures also infused nature and common-place natural events with god-like attributes. Primitive societies even today demonstrate a similar propensity to invest animate and inanimate objects with godlike or spiritual presence and force in order to establish physical connection with the spirit or invisible world.

Little changed in the nature of religious understanding over the next thousands of years because mankind's scientific understanding of the true nature of the universe increased very little during that time. Indeed, in some civilizations, such as ancient Egypt, it did not change at all. The high, later civilizations of Persia, Greece, and Rome, still based much of their religious belief on superstition and personal conceptions of gods. Even Christianity and Islam adapted their dogma and rituals to incorporate many pagan beliefs into their own religious practices. Moreover, the hierarchal structures of the Catholic and Islamic organizations resisted challenge to dogma because of the perceived threat that such challenges posed to their power and the well-founded concern that the change of the popular understanding of the physical nature of the world would result in the loss of faith in the masses over whom they exerted almost complete dominion.

It was only with the slow employment of the scientific method for examining, discovering, and conceptualizing a more accurate nature of reality did mankind gain an opportunity to challenge the dual universe ideology and form a better, truer understanding of existence and the nature of the relationship between mankind and the universe, and, of course, ultimately, God. At long last, after centuries of darkness and erroneous understanding, mankind is on the precipice of developing a true "religion" based upon a genuine conception of existence, the universe and most importantly, God.

Thus, a genuine religion is ready to be born based upon a non-mythic, scientific understanding of Nature and the Universe. With each day , it seems, scientists uncover more details or visions of the physical universe that clarifies or debunks prior understanding, and on and on it goes, with the hope that someday, a theory of everything, including God perhaps, will be determined.

For thousands of years, mankind has believed that there were two planes of existence - a visible one in which everyday action took place, and a greater, much more powerful invisible or supernatural one, upon which the visible one depended, and from which it drew its powers. According to this worldview, the predicament of life is to control and tap the powers of the invisible, spirit world. From the earliest times, this has been the function of the religious practitioner or priest who was thought to be endowed with the ability of bridging the two planes of existence, natural and supernatural/heaven and earth. Modern science has not debunked this view, and in some ways, enhanced the belief in the existence of a dual natural and supernatural reality. Thus, if a genuine religion comes to pass that includes a belief in God and the supernatural as an element of reality, it can find support for such ideas in modern scientific theory.

After years of rejecting the possible existence of the spirit world, and God, based upon the rush of cold, scientific discovery, sentiment has been growing in recent years among scientists that a complete and accurate understanding of Nature must be wedded to a religious or spiritual component. Indeed, the recent discoveries in quantum physics, and in the field of cosmology, have left many credible scientists with the awestruck sense that leaving out a spiritual component regarding the nature of existence is itself unscientific. Thus, there is a movement among many such scientists for a unified theory of existence that incorporates spiritual and religious as well of purely scientific components.

Modern science demonstrates that the commonsense post-Enlightenment view of reality is not "the truth". There is, empirically, an invisible nature of microcosmic and cosmic levels demonstrating that the "stuff" of existence is in many ways ephemeral and supernatural. Reality thus includes the here and now of the natural universe, as well as a supernatural plane that only further scientific discovery can hope to comprehend.

In short, the more scientists learn, the closer they feel to God!

(B). The Effect of the Repudiation of One's Reality

Isaac Asimov's classic short story, *Nightfall*, explored the awful destructive power unleashed among sentient beings when they are suddenly and starkly awakened to the falsity of the reality upon which their civilization, and therefore, hero systems, has been built.

The story concerns the coming of darkness due to the rare eclipse of the sun of the planet, Lagash, which normally illuminates the planet at all times thus hiding stars from view. Indeed, due to Lagash's complete illumination at all times, total darkness is unknown, and thus, its people are unaware of the existence of the larger universe consisting of billions of stars and galaxies of stars. "Nightfall" occurs once every 2,049 years, when the sun on one side of the planet is eclipsed for half a day by a planet whose existence has been inferred by scientists. Past occurrences of the nightfall event had purportedly coincided with the collapse of Lagashian civilization, which has risen and fallen close to a dozen times, since the darkness results in madness and panic among Lagash's populace.

The story deals with the conflicting agendas of scientists - including astronomers and a psychologist - who wish to understand and explain the phenomenon for future generations, and "Cultists" whose holy book contains an apocalyptic account of "Darkness" and "Stars" from the last occurrence and who welcome it as a spiritual event. The central character is a journalist who is at first skeptical that the event will even take place but soon becomes enthralled by the possibility.

The story climaxes with the onset of nightfall, demonstrating that the understanding of reality is completely wrong, thus rendering meaningless the primary beliefs of the current Lagashian culture which have been built upon that reality. The result is the repeat of the collapse of the present civilization. The story concludes as follows:

With the slow fascination of fear, he lifted himself on one arm and turned his eyes toward the blood-curdling blackness of the window.

Through it shone the Stars! Not Earth's feeble thirty-six hundred Stars visible to the eye; Lagash was in the center of a giant cluster. Thirty thousand mighty suns shone down in a soul-searing splendor that was more frighteningly cold in its awful indifference than the bitter wind that shivered across the cold, horribly bleak world.

Theremon staggered to his feet, his throat, constricting him to breathlessness, all the muscles of his body writhing in an intensity of terror and sheer fear beyond bearing. He was going mad and knew it, and somewhere deep inside a bit of sanity was screaming, struggling to fight off the hopeless flood of black terror. It was very horrible to go mad and know that you were going mad -- to know that in a little minute you would be here physically and yet all the real essence would be dead and drowned in the black madness. For this was the Dark -- the Dark and the Cold and the Doom. The bright walls of the universe were shattered and their awful black fragments were falling down to crush and squeeze and obliterate him.

He jostled someone crawling on hands and knees, but stumbled somehow over him. Hands groping at his tortured throat, he limped toward the flame of the torches that filled all his mad vision.

'Light!' he screamed.

Aton, somewhere, was crying, whimpering horribly like a terribly frightened child. 'Stars -- all the Stars -- we didn't know at all. We didn't know anything. We thought six stars in a universe is something the Stars didn't notice is Darkness forever and ever and ever and the walls are breaking in and we didn't know we couldn't know and anything -- 'Someone clawed at the torch, and it fell and snuffed out. In the instant, the awful splendor of the indifferent Stars leaped nearer to them.

On the horizon outside the window, in the direction of Saro City, a crimson glow began growing, strengthening in brightness, that was not the glow of a sun.

The long night had come again.

The lesson of this story is twofold: first, that our conception of reality may be incorrect because we have an mistaken and/or incomplete scientific understanding of the nature of the universe; and, second, that when such lack of understanding is revealed to us, we either reject the truth and elect to ignore it and go on believing something that is false (like the Lagashian "Cultist"), or we collapse into depression or madness.

The experience of the Lagashians, whose reality was suddenly revealed to them as false, is evident in modern society although by less drastic means and with less destructive results. With the explosion of scientific knowledge over the past 250 years, the old mythical religious beliefs, such as Christianity, Islam and Hinduism, have been shown to be based on an erroneous understanding of Nature and reality. Like the inhabitants of Lagash in *Nightfall*, the stars have come out to reveal to modern humans that the cosmological understanding of the ancient religions of Christianity, Islam and Hinduism is in a physical, if not spiritual, sense erroneous.

Nevertheless, a high percentage of humans still refuse to reject or discard their faith in these religions. Unable to adhere to these beliefs in the face of scientific knowledge, many others have drifted into depression and mental illness, or adopted immoral or equally meaningless and trivial, un-real forms of beliefs in the formation of their life immorality elusions to gain relief from the death/meaninglessness anxiety.

Unfortunately, modern science has as of yet been unable to articulate a definitive conception of the universe, based upon experiment and observation, and scientists have even admitted that they are far from being able to do so, if ever at all. So we are left with mere speculation on the part of even the most brilliant scientists and cosmologists about the nature of the Cosmos and God, or if such an entity even exists. In face of the terror of death, the burden for some persons of an unknown and possibly unknowable God is too great. The void has thus been filled in modern cultures by hero systems causing materialistic, hedonistic, immoral, trivial and sometimes violent behavior.

However, the answer is not yet more false religion built on disprovable myth, but upon the articulation and establishment of a new, modern religion which embraces the human quest for an understanding how nature works, and, ultimately, the nature of God.

(C). Accepting Reality

What if a person could accept that life is defined by only two realities – existence and death, and that all motivations were mere based upon mere constructs, created among the minds of human beings to hide the fact of the second reality, death?

Ernest Becker speculated that by acknowledging the reality of death might render a person mentally unstable, incapable of action, utterly stricken by the terror of that realization. Alternatively, such a person might be invigorated by the sense of freedom and relief granted by the sincere acceptance of death and the concomitant realization that one's life has been built on a meaningless or unimportant illusion constructed solely to hide the reality of death. It is likely that such a person would suffer both consequences – mental imbalance and euphoria - in varying degrees, at varying times, just as periodically experienced by his counterpart embedded and operating under the constructs of modern cultural hero systems.

Thus, the terror of death ironically benefits mankind because it forces him to create systems of belief, and action, to overcome that terror. The shortcomings of the devises humanity uses to do so is what has led it down a such dismal, violent and ignorant historic path in which the species has failed to achieve its potential.

The popular *Matrix* movie series provides insight into one's ability to transcend the false perception of reality imposed by the socialization process by boldly accepting the truth of its falsity. The main character, Neo, becomes totally free, and literally gains the ability to soar above the clouds and fly like a superman when he accepts that the world in which he has been living is in fact, a construct, a symbolic, fictitious simulation of reality imbedded in his mind by machines who require the energy of the human body to fuel their technological existence. The movie demonstrates that acceptance of the falsity of one's reality is sublimely difficult, but once gained, empowers the person like nothing else.

But toward what end? In *The Matrix* series, Neo succeeds in staving off annihilation for those humans who have awakened from the machine driven dreams of life. That is his mission, his quest. However, once that is achieved, there is peaceful harmony, a balance for the time being, but there is the implication at the end of the last sequel, *Matrix Revolutions,* that the machines are ready to construct yet another, inevitable, and possibly pure construct.

Thus, the *Matrix* demonstrates that when we cast aside the symbolic trappings of our heroism, and accept the real nature of the world, we are empowered to control our own destiny – we can fly through the air like supermen! We can escape the false and ultimately debilitating symbolism of the construct world, and embark on a quest to discover truth.

Similarly, this Manifesto posits an escape from the spiritually, intellectually and emotionally debilitating illusions which modern cultures offer through the socialization process for the purpose of denying the reality of life and death. Escaping the illusion of modern life is accomplished by simply accepting that fact – that life is a culturally programmed illusion, a flight from death. Then, once the person is awakened to that realization, he or she will construct what Becker termed, an "ideal illusion" based upon reality of life and death motivating heroic endeavors that advance the quality of life for all members of the cultural group, that enhance the eternal survival of the human species, and that foster a genuine comprehension of God and the nature of the Cosmos.

Chapter Eight
Epilogue: An Explanation for the Failure of Humanity

What the anthropologists call 'cultural relativity' is thus really the relativity of hero-systems the world over. But each cultural system is a dramatization of earthly heroics; each system cuts out roles for performances of various degrees of heroism: from the 'high' heroism of a Churchill, a Mao, or a Buddha, to the 'low' heroism of the coal miner, the peasant, the simple priest; the plain, everyday earthly heroism wrought by gnarled working hands guiding a family through hunger and disease.
- Ernest Becker

The preceding pages have attempted to explain why humanity has failed to achieve its spiritual, intellectual and technological potential despite its vast intelligence, especially after the agricultural revolution and the advent of civilization. Such failure is directly related to the insufficient or deficient methods offered among cultures to enable their members to repress the psychological anxiety caused by the consciousness of death and concomitant concept of meaningless which such consciousness inspires. Human beings construct illusions that hide the fact of death; however, such illusions fail to stave off the nagging realization of death and annihilation, and attempt to do so in ways that are trivial and destructive and ultimately are inimical to human advancement and survival.

The consciousness of death and anxiety or terror such consciousness inspires, which is the motivating force for human behavior, can be displayed by the following equation:

Awareness of Death = Fear/Anxiety of Death = Need to Repress Fear/Anxiety of Death = Symbolic methods, offered by cultural hero systems, for Repression of Fear/Anxiety of Death = Construction of LIEs = Self-Esteem = Human Behavior.

Given that the historical record, and news of today, amply demonstrate that cultural hero systems inspire humans more often than to commit despicable, violent and stupid acts which have markedly failed to create an enlightened and unified species that affords an optimum quality of life for all its members; that has utterly failed to enhance, let alone insure, the survivability of the species from extinction by natural or man-made cataclysm; and, that continues to accept a puerile and purely mythical description for God and the Cosmos, this Manifesto explains that the cause of such regrettable human behavior are deficient cultural hero systems. Thus, a hero system needs to be designed and then offered to cultural members which motivates them to act in ways that provide for the highest quality of life for all its members; that insures the survivability of the species; and, that fosters a genuine comprehension of God and the Cosmos.

The remainder of this Manifesto will attempt to describe such a hero system, termed the *Genuine Hero System*, which it is hoped will become the blueprint for a future society of mankind that recognizes the sacred nature of the human species and therefore seeks justice and plenty for all its members as well as its own eternal salvation, and which compels its members to embark on the long and necessary quest for a real comprehension of God's place in the lives of men, and mankind's place in the Cosmos.

So let us begin....

PART TWO

AN IDEAL ILLUSION:
THE GENUINE HERO SYSTEM

*… if everyone honestly admitted his urge to be a hero it would be
a devastating release of truth. It would make men demand that
culture give them their due – a primary sense of human value
as unique contributors to cosmic life. How would our modern
societies contrive to satisfy such an honest demand, without being
shaken to their very foundation? Only those societies we today call
"primitive" provided this feeling for their members.*

*If transference is a natural function of heroism,
a necessary projection in order to stand life, death, and oneself, the
question becomes: which is creative projection?
Which is life-enhancing illusion?*
- Ernest Becker

*A truly intelligent species must have the ability to behave,
collectively, in ways that ensure long-term survival.
It must have learned to avoid natural disaster…*
- David Grinspoon

CHAPTER NINE
THE GENUINE HERO SYSTEM

...you have to actually set up some kind of liberating ideal,
some kind of life-giving alternative to the thoughtless and
destructive heroism; you have to begin to scheme to give to man
an opportunity for heroic victory that is not a simple reflex of
narcissistic scapegoating.
- Ernest Becker

He who does not really feel himself lost, is without remission;
that is to say, he never finds himself, never comes up against his
own reality.
- Jose Ortega

(A). The Life Immortality Elusion (LIE); Character as The
Vital Lie

Everyone's behavior – what each of us do in our
lives - is motivated by what this Manifesto has termed
one's, "Life Immortality Elusion" or "LIE." (What Ernest
Becker called the life immortality project or the vital lie
of character). LIEs are symbolic illusions constructed by
individuals from methods offered by cultural hero systems

in furtherance of the psychological process of denying the reality of death. One's LIE accomplishes this by instilling a facade of symbolic self-esteem through the activities of everyday life, and a connection to personal immortality by adopting a belief in supernatural existence supported by religious or spiritual myth.

A person's LIE is constructed from an array of methods for that purpose which have arisen in the culture in which he or she resides, based upon that the evolution over time of that culture's social-economic, political and religious beliefs. The express purpose of such beliefs is to supply the members of the culture with vehicles for gaining self-esteem, and a connection to supernatural existence beyond the physical, visible realm – that is, an afterlife and immortality, in a concerted, psychologically driven, purposeful effort among its members to enable them to repress or overcome the terror raised by the prospect of eventual and inevitable death.

In short, one's LIE is constructed for the sole and necessary purpose of creating an illusion of meaning to overcome the reality of death.

(B). The Failure of Humanity

It is self-evident that the human species has failed to reach its highest spiritual, intellectual and technological potential. Indeed, a review of human history reflects that humanity is a failed species continuously mired in violent internecine clashes and inexplicably incapable of providing sufficient sustenance, shelter, and other basic life needs and requirements essential for the pursuit of happiness to the great majority of its members despite the obvious fact that humanity has the clear ability to do so. Instead, the species wastes its considerable   mental, physical and financial resources on trivial, violent or other pursuits inimical to the individual and collective pursuit of life, liberty and happiness.

To this day, there continues to be violent clashes among nations, tribes, families, gangs, and all type of other cultural and sub-cultural groups; inharmonious relations within and without societies; the expenditure of vast physical, mental and financial resources on weaponry and other materials, services, and activities in pursuit of wasteful, banal or trivial matters which bear absolutely no relationship to improving the material, spiritual and intellectual quality of life for all human beings, and enhancing the long-range survivability of the species. Moreover, these expenditures of thought, money and spirit bear no relationship or nexus to the reality of existence, but instead are designed to promulgate, among other things, nationalism, materialism, or religious ideology which form the basis for the death denying illusions, by way of the life immortality projects or elusions, of the masses.

The shortcomings of humanity, illustrated by the indictment set forth in Chapter One, are directly related to two factors. First, the old beliefs offered by past and modern cultures are no longer accepted as accurate depictions of reality and thus the actions motivated by them fail to instill in the individual a sense of self-esteem or faith in personal immortality. Second, even those religious and non-religious beliefs that continue to motivate human action do say in ways that are destructive, inappropriate, insufficient, and wasteful. What is needed is a radical change of the belief system that acts as the motivating force for human behavior.

As Barbara Dewey put it in *As You Believe*

Humans and animals must feel the exhilaration of personal accomplishment.

They must experience their own effectiveness – their personal ability to make a difference. Without an outlet to demonstrate such effectiveness, the will to live will be severely threatened...Welfare rolls, alcoholism, drug addition, suicide rates, highway fatalities, the so-called breakdown of moral fiber – all attest to a society which, for too many, does not offer the means to a satisfactory expression of purpose...The societal breakdown is largely due, I believe, to a state of transition in which we, as a culture, find ourselves. We move from the 19th century purposes which are no longer relevant in the latter part of the 20th century, to 21st century purposes which are not yet in place.

It is the intention of this Manifesto to inspire all humans to rethink the methods employed that give their lives meaning and purpose and to offer those purposes to which they should aspire based upon the beliefs underlying the Genuine Hero System.

(C). <u>The Genuine Hero System As The Motivational Force</u>

The central purpose of this *Manifesto* is to awaken humanity to the extreme failure of its past and present cultures in providing human beings with bona fide means for confronting the fear of death in a genuine or meaningful way. It also seeks to highlight the failure mankind's cultural hero systems in enhancing the possibility of the eternal survival of the human species and in advocating methods for motivating positive human behaviors which genuinely increase the quality of life and possibility of liberty and happiness for everyone, as well as advancing the survivability of the species.

The essential problem, then, comes down to not only convincing mankind to abandon its failed methods for attaining heroism in the task of denying death, but also in finding the right kind of heroism that will achieve these goals.　Humans must recognize the futility of their present life illusions, that their life projects are ultimately false methods of attaining release from the reality of death, and come to adopt wholly new methods for doing so.　They must discard their present LIEs, and formulate new LIEs, which Becker termed, ideal illusions, which directs their lives in service of their fellow man so as to enhance the quality of life for others and increase the prospect of the survival of the human species.

This Manifesto prescribes a model for cultural heroism, termed the "Genuine Hero System," offering action methods precisely designed to increase the quality of life for all humans, to enhance the potential for the survival of the human species, and to seek the true or absolute comprehension of God and the Cosmos.　Only by instituting such system among human cultures will mankind reach its highest spiritual, intellectual and technological potential and thus achieve the promise of eternal survival for the species and a comprehension of God and the Cosmos.　Conversely, unless humanity alters its methods of constructing illusions that deny death, as Becker feared, the species is doomed to extinction.

So how is the Genuine Hero System different than past and present hero systems?　What are its foundational beliefs and what methods does it offer individuals for constructing life illusions that enable them to attain self-worth and a communion or covenant with God and the Cosmos?

The Genuine Hero System is based upon an abiding belief in the sanctity of life and humanity as a sacred creature of the universe.　The essential belief underlying the Genuine Hero System, its religion, if you will, is that mankind is a sacred evolutionary product of the wonder of Life.　Under this humanist ideology, the evolution of life is seen as a universal or cosmic urge to embrace or approach God. Humanity is deemed an significant if not ultimate step in that blessed evolution. The Genuine Hero System is thus designed to motivate action methods that assist humanity in its evolutionary duty of approaching God through comprehension of what God and the Cosmos are. The role of species is to survive, of course, and those species that attain consciousness have the added function of furthering life by reaching a comprehension or even an accommodation with God.

In furthering this essential function of a consciously evolved animal, The Genuine Hero System proposes methods for constructing a life immortality elusion for self-esteem creation that is based on beliefs of the sanctity of humanity that compel basic service to the collective good, and that enhance the survival of the individual and group. In addition, the Genuine Hero System also directs behavior that enables adherents to better comprehend the nature of God and the Cosmic Entity. A member of a culture that has adopted the Genuine Hero System is driven to action resulting in the enrichment of individual dignity and enhancement of the quality of life for all humans, while also serving the collective good of the species by advancing the promise of its eternal survival, and the related spiritual, intellectual and technological progress of the species. He or she is also driven to embark upon a quest, through spiritual and intellectual contemplation, and scientific discovery, that enables mankind to approach a comprehension of God and the Cosmos.

In sum, under the Genuine Hero System, individual self-esteem is predicated upon achievements which promote both the quality of life of other individuals in the cultural group and the survival of the species as well as furthering the collective human quest for a comprehension of God and the Cosmos.

(D). The Quest for A Comprehension of God

As will be further detailed in the next chapter, a cornerstone of the Genuine Hero System proposed by this Manifesto is a genuine and sincere belief in some kind of God. Indeed, unless the person comes to adopt that belief, relief from death anxiety through heroic action is unattainable. Simply put, to lead a normal and contented life immersed in an ideal illusion constructed from the methods offered by the Genuine Hero System, one must believe in the existence of God and the promise of personal immortality.

However, the need for the person to embrace the idea of the existence of God must be coupled with the sincere and whole-hearted recognition that comprehension of God, and the nature of Universe, is vastly incomplete at the present stage of human intellectual and spiritual development (due, in large part, to the lack of sufficient human organization and advancement under the pre-existing false cultural hero systems which dominate present human cultures). Thus, rejecting one's current life immortality illusion necessarily involves a rejection of one's religious faith. If one is a Christian or Muslim, in order to join a Genuine Hero System culture, he or she must withdraw allegiance and adherence to those faiths.

This Manifesto further postulates that humans have an innate drive to connect with and comprehend the very nature of God and the Cosmos. Under the GHS, that drive is allowed to flower into a scientific, intellectual and spiritual quest.

(E). Summary

Humanity must accept and learn from its failure as a sentient species to have reached its highest spiritual, intellectual and technological potential. This Manifesto argues that such failure is attributable to the methods offered by past and present cultures to its members for constructing symbolic illusions to obscure the reality of death.

The Genuine Hero System is based upon the paradoxical recognition that death is real, but that an illusion of the symbolic meaning of life is needed to obscure that reality; and, that such heroic illusion, in order to avoid the extinction and continued misery of the majority of the members of the human species, must be constructed from methods of heroism that improve the lives of other cultural members; that enhance the survivability of the human species; and, that compel a quest for a comprehension of the genuine nature of God and the Cosmos.

CHAPTER TEN
THE VITAL ROLE OF BELIEF IN GOD

The heavens declare the glory of God;
the skies proclaim the work of His hands.
- Psalm 19

The experience of moksha would then consist of the blissful
awareness that our existence is not separate and isolated, but one
with ultimate reality...There is no separate identity or ego.
The ego's impression of a distinct identityis an illusion...
our suffering has no independent reality.
- John F. Haught

(A). <u>General Principles</u>

A primary message of this *Manifesto* is that the religious beliefs offered by past and present cultural hero systems have failed to adequately define God's function as a part of reality and the role which God plays in the lives of men. Although mankind's religions may in some sense symbolically or archetypically describe the nature of reality, they present inadequate or completely erroneous renditions of that reality, and therefore advocate a mistaken description of the true nature of God and the Cosmos.

The historic religions, such as Judaism, Christianity and Islam, are based upon mere superstition or inaccurate and false conceptions of the physical and natural universe. They present cosmologies that are counter to the present understanding of the universe by the current level of scientific assessment and theory. Religious beliefs have thus been formed around purely mythical or symbolic and unscientific conceptions of God and Nature that are simply uninformed fictions or stories. Religions are based on myth, not scientific or intellectual truth, and that is ultimately the essential flaw in maintaining them as viable beliefs upon which to base methods of action.

Past cultures were able to furnish their members with a means for overcoming the death/meaninglessness anxiety through the religious beliefs offered in their symbolic hero systems because of the lack of scientific understanding of Cosmos. However, the past 250 years has seen a rapid and dramatic increase in scientific discovery resulting in a significantly better understanding of the true nature of the Universe. In addition, there have been substantial advancements in areas of intellectual, spiritual and philosophical thought. Through the confluence of science and the enlightenment of thought, the basic tenets of the old religions have been shown to be seriously flawed in not entirely debunked.

However, in the process of debunking the ancient precepts which served as the foundation for the ancient religions, science has failed to articulate a coherent supernatural alternative which can be used by modern man to fill the void. Thus, modern man has been left with a substantial void in a crucial belief for repression of the death/meaninglessness anxiety. This void goes a long way in explaining modern man's apparent lack of a moral center, mental instability, and obsession with trivial and sometimes perverse pursuits and interests.

As stated previously, there is an vital and necessary place for belief in God in the Genuine Hero System. Belief in a God concept, however that term is ultimately defined, is indispensable to a healthy-minded life free from the psychologically debilitating terror of death. One must attain a secure level of faith in God's existence and one's possible immortality stemming from that faith to function optimally in everyday life.

Hence, except for an under-educated, misguided or brainwashed segment of the human population, the religious beliefs offered by modern cultures have failed to furnish a considerable number of humans with a valid and supportable sense of, or connection with, a concept of God as a relevant motivational force and factor in their lives. Stated another way, modern religion has failed to provide countless millions of human beings with a sense of understanding of God sufficient to satisfy the basic need for a personal link to an existence beyond the physical realm. This absence of a basis for faith has resulted in despair and longing, greatly enhanced the individual's death/meaningless anxiety and inspired the pursuit of trivial activities and beliefs inimical to human advancement. In sum, the lack of genuine faith in a true God has contributed to modern humanity's penchant for immorality and evil behavior.

Ernest Becker recognized that the individual has two primary ontological needs in order to become happy and fulfilled in the process of overcoming or repressing the death/meaninglessness anxiety:

First, he must attain a sense of self-esteem

constructed from his or her contribution to the cultural group and sub-group in which he or she resides fostered by the heroic methods offered by that culture's hero system based upon its political, social, economic and religious beliefs. As has been previously argued, these methods are ingrained upon the psyche of the individual through the socialization process. One achieves a measure of self-worth or self-esteem by acting in furtherance of these methodological templates.

However, gaining self-esteem via the methods offered by one's cultural hero system is simply not enough for the individual to overcome the death/meaningless anxiety. Beyond attaining personal self-esteem in the physical, "everyday" sphere, the individual must also acquire faith in the promise of personal immortality in a supernatural realm governed by some perceptible God concept or force. Indeed, religious beliefs arose among cultural groups primarily for the purpose of providing such promise and link to a tangible God figure in order to explain away the stark problem of death. These beliefs solved the problem of where the person goes after death. For example, Christianity promises immortality to those who obey certain moral laws in a Heaven ruled by Jesus Christ, the purported Son of God, following the mythical Christ figure's Second Coming.

Thus, in addition to offering methods for individual self-esteem by quantifiable and qualifiable accomplishments in the physical realm, cultural hero systems must offer methods, through religious beliefs, which enable the person to achieve and maintain the promise of personal immortality in the supernatural realm.

The problem for the modern human is that over the past 250 some odd years, scientific examination and discovery have largely debunked the mythical cosmologies underlying historical religious beliefs, such as Christianity and Islam, which have been offered as the means to satisfying the promise of immortality by cultural hero systems for thousands of years. The earth has been shown to orbit the sun in what we now call the solar system. And it has been demonstrated that the solar system itself, though spread out over vast distances from the human perspective, is a mere infinitesimal speck in the whole order of the incomprehensibly immense universe of stars, galaxies and light and dark matter that is spread across the sky, it is estimated, for a distance of at least 14 billion light years.

Furthermore, science has demonstrated that rather than being created by an Supreme Act of an involved God, as stated in the Old Testament and other ancient religious tomes, mankind's existence, and the existence of all life, is the product of evolution, a kind of precise, mechanical design of Nature through the agency of natural selection and genetic mutation. However, such design appears to be dispassionate, and there is no proof, one way or another, that it has an Intelligent or Supernatural author. Evolution is natural process, like the birth and death of stars, planets, galaxies, and perhaps universe, a kind of algorithm that propels life, once it comes into being, to change over time based upon various complex, environmental and other factors usually into higher forms of animate existence. However, there is no proof for a so-called "Intelligent Design" directing or even remotely interested in such evolutionary process as it has worked on the earth.

Science has thus called into serious question the antiquated methods the ancient religions offered for promising immortality through their various conceptualizations of God. While some scholars have argued that the Old Testament and other religious writings remain viable and relevant as symbolic representations of modern scientific findings, for many, if not most modern, educated humans, scientific discovery has rendered the God of the Old, and even New, Testaments largely irrelevant whose dogma and ritual are more to be tolerated than believed.

Thus, the basic theologies underlying the great religions have been seriously cast into doubt and, at very least, if not altogether discarded, seem to require a significant reformulation to have some relevance in the modern age. Indeed, the rise of atheism as espoused by intellectuals and scientists such as Richard Dawkins, Sam Harris, and Richard Dennett, are based in part on the idea that science has rendered belief in God as wholly irrational and misguided. These scholars argue, often rightly, that the old religious beliefs are no longer relevant and useful, except for the dull-witted, to explain cosmological purpose, and indeed foster evil and destructive behavior in furtherance of their respective outmoded creeds and dogmas especially when they clash with other cultures.

However, below the surface of these doubts in the efficacy of the old religions lurks the sense that rather than disproving the existence of God, modern scientific discovery has merely altered mankind's comprehension of what God is, and what His/Her role in the universe must be. At very least, modern scientific understanding has demonstrated that humanity does not yet possess a clear, unambiguous and meaningful comprehension of God and the natural universe. Modern science teaches that the profound and difficult cosmological questions remain unanswered and for some, may be unanswerable.

In sum, the scientific answers to the riddle of God's existence and the nature of the Cosmos is a work-in-progress. On the basis of what we know about the nature of the universe, through such scientific examination and discovery, no one can say with any legitimate and credible certainly whether or not God exists, and anyone proclaiming otherwise is simply engaging in demagoguery. Stated another way, we do not yet have a complete understanding regarding the nature of Nature, and hence, cannot have a complete understanding regarding the existence and nature of God. Our descriptions of God and the afterlife are mere conjecture, from whatever source they have been attempted, religious, atheistic intellectual, spiritual, philosophical or otherwise.

Some might argue that this position – that we do not yet have an answer to the question of God's existence, nature and relationship with the universe and humanity, does nothing to alleviate the death/meaninglessness anxiety. Saying that God's existence is an open question, leaves open the possibility that the atheists are right, that God does not exist, and that human life is therefore a seemingly pointless inter-reaction of molecules in a complex cosmic chemical process. However, there are many scientists who believe that modern findings regarding the nature of the universe strongly favor the existence of God, or some kind of "intelligent design" or purpose underlying universal occurrences.

As Becker realized and articulated, in order to live harmoniously and healthily, in psychological terms, in the face of one's impending and inevitable death, belief in God's existence is absolutely and profoundly essential. The culture which does not offer a religious belief component or opportunity to adopt a belief in God, will be doomed to wither and eventually perish. Indeed, communist based cultures have largely substantiated this position. Simply put, a God-less culture can never hope to produce happy and contented members because without the prospect or hope of immortality in an even faulty mythological cosmologi͏ and supernatural construct ruled over by some God, the death/meaningless anxiety for such members can never be adequately repressed or overcome, and the individual's life will be at least subconsciously riddled with doubt and fear.

Thus, the Genuine Hero System appreciates the paramount need for offering a religious belief or theory to its adherents. Therefore, faith in God, and immortal existence, is a primary and perhaps most important component of such system. However, such Faith must be based on truth, not some new mythological construct designed and promulgated simply to provide a person with the fake promise of immortality in a supernatural realm.

This Manifesto suggests that Genuine Hero System can actually offer two arguments for adopting faith in God which can alleviate, if not obviate, the individual's death/meaningless anxiety.

First, a person can simply accept, as many scientists have, that the scientific discoveries of modern times, especially in the last 250 years, actually demonstrate the existence of a force, essence, or presence underlying the Cosmos which implies the existence of God. Under this scenario, a belief can be constructed that there is more to existence than what is apparent in the physical realm and that therefore, death is not the end of life, but merely a transformation into a new form of being, and that one's existence is therefore truly eternal.

Second, and alternatively, a person can simply leave the question open, unanswered, neither admitting nor denying the existence of God, but rather keeping an open mind that God might be behind the forces making up the physical realm of the Cosmos, and that death may not be the end of one's essence and being.

In either case, the religious component of the

Genuine Hero System is built around the principle that we should direct our spiritual energy and resources toward gaining a complete comprehension of God and the Cosmos whether the purpose of such quest be to determine the existence of God or to better comprehend the nature of the God whose existence is taken for granted.

Based upon either the acceptance of the reality of God, or the possibility of that reality, the religion of mankind should simply become a quest for God. Humanity should at very least accept that we have not gained a sufficient understanding of what God is, and then embark on a profound and, if necessary, eternal mission to do so.

(B). <u>The Question of God's Existence</u>

There have been myriad books written debating whether God exists or whether the existence of God can be proven. Many authors with diverse backgrounds and motivations, including holy men, priests, shamans, scientists, philosophers, layman, mathematicians, prophets, mad men and others, have chimed in on this important though difficult and slippery topic over the centuries of human history. Since the dawn of history, numerous cogent and profound arguments for and against the existence of God and a deistic creative force underlying the physical universe have been advanced.

The simple point is that the study of all that has ever been said or written on the topic of God and the nature of the Cosmos brings no clear and satisfying conclusion to the question of God's existence. At least based upon the current state of human knowledge, whether of not God really exists, or the essence of his being, cannot be conclusively demonstrated either way.

But so what? That lack of a definitive answer does

not mean that there is no God. It only means that at our present level of study and comprehension, we as a species have been unable to determine a coherent, genuine answer to the perplexing questions of God's existence and nature. We can only conclude with any amount of certainty that more study on the topic of God and the nature of the Cosmos is left to be done.

While this writer has chosen to believe that there is some intelligent force behind the marvelous mechanics evident in the physical universe – termed for purposes of this discussion, a God Concept or Force (although the movie, Star Wars, has given the idea of a God as a spiritual "Force" a kind of comical or corny meaning), it is not necessary in order to satisfy the "Beyond" component in the construction of one's LIE to have attained an absolute and unshakable Faith in God. All one needs is to do is accept the possibility of God's existence together with an avid thirst for more information and knowledge regarding the question. It is the further belief of this writer that the more knowledge is gained, and the longer humanity embarks on this quest to find God, the more certain we will all become that a God of some kind truly does exist.

However, one must acknowledge that, no matter what has been written, and what reasoned arguments have been made pro or con, we simply do not know at this point in time in human history the essence of God's being (or as indicated above, for some at least, whether God truly exists at all). And in making this concession, the Genuine Hero System suggests that the person should be able to join the sublime quest in answer to the riddle of God. This Manifesto submits that this is all a human being need to do in order to satisfy his or her spiritual longing in the face of death. The death/meaningless anxiety can be at least quelled, if not wholly silenced, in joining the quest to obtain a genuine comprehension of God and the Cosmos.

Of course, this is no real substitute for gaining a sense of Faith that God does in fact exist, and that personal immortality is really in the cards, that it is part of the reality of existence. However, it is the fervent belief of this writer that as mankind genuinely and enthusiastically pursues the quest for God, He will at some point reveal Himself to the species and to individual members.

(C). The Case For God

A considerable number of distinguished scientists and thinkers are willing to go beyond merely admitting the possibility of God's existence. Rather, they profess that such existence has already been demonstrated, to their ultimate satisfaction, and that it is based upon existing scientifically proven fact and intellectual understanding. (Of course, there is the contrary faction which just as adamantly argues that God's existence has been disproved by scientific study. However, this writer submits that neither faction can convincingly prove its case – either for or against the existence and being of God).

In *The Language of God,* for instance, famed human genome project biologist, Francis S. Collins, cites The Moral Law as proof for the existence of God, that is, the universality of the concept of right and wrong behavior that is present across human cultures both past and present and which applies peculiarly to human beings. The Moral Law uniformly decries and condemns oppression, murder, treachery and falsehood. It is especially embodied in the altruistic impulse, the "self-less" love known as, *agape.* Collins pointedly argues that although the Moral Law and altruism serve no evolutionary survival purpose, they are evidence of a higher force beyond natural laws.

Most scientists agree, at least at the time of the writing of this *Manifesto,* that the Big Bang theory explains the creation of the universe in which human beings exist. It is a complicated and difficult, if not incomprehensible, explanation for the ordinary human mind to grasp, at least at this juncture in humanity's intellectual and scientific development. Nevertheless, even with our limited understanding of the actual mechanics underlying the Big Bang, many scientists argue that the fact that the universe formed in exactly the way it did which was precisely what was necessary for life to arise is further evidence of divine presence, if not design.

Collins writes that the physical manifestation of our Universe is "wildly improbable." He goes on to cite the following statement of most famous theoretical physicist of our day, Stephen Hawking: "The odds against a universe like ours emerging out of something like the Big Bang are enormous. I think there are clearly religious implications." In *A Brief History of Time*, Hawking added: "It would be very difficult to explain why the universe should have begun in just this way, except as the act of a God who intended to create beings like us."

In *A Short History of Nearly Everything,* generalist, Bill Bryson, eloquently and insightfully described existence in the moment of time and space before the Big Bang resulted in the creation of the rest of the universe, an event he termed "the singularity":

> *It is natural but wrong to visualize the singularity as a kind of pregnant dot hanging in a dark, boundless void. But there is no space, no darkness. The singularity has no "around" around it. There is no space for it to occupy; no place for it to*

be. We can't even ask how long it has been there – whether it has just lately popped into being, like a good idea, or whether it has been there forever, quietly awaiting the right moment. Time doesn't exist. There is no past for it to emerge from.

And with poetic flourish, Bryson remarks:

And so, from nothing, our universe begins.

And he goes on to describe with utter clarity the moment of the Big Bang itself:

In a single blinding pulse, a moment of glory much too swift and expansive for any form of words, the singularity assumes heavenly dimensions, space beyond conception.

Bryson likewise propounds the idea that unless the universe was formed in just a certain way, the universe and mankind would not have come into being. He writes:

What is extraordinary from our point of view is how well it turned out for us. If the universe had formed just a tiny bit differently – if gravity were fractionally stronger or weaker, if the expansion had proceeded just a little more slowly or swiftly – then there might never have been stable elements to make you and me and the ground we stand on. Had gravity been a trifle stronger, the universe itself might have collapsed like a badly erected tent, without precisely the right values to give it the right dimensions and density and component parts. Had it been weaker, however, nothing would have coalesced. The universe would have remained forever a dull, scattered void.

In sum, many scientists believe that these mathematically improbable occurrences resulting in the universal soup which followed the Big Bang that was just right to result in mankind is definitive evidence of a purpose governing the creation and development of the Universe in which we live and, hence, of some kind of God or force or whatever you want to call it behind it all. It gives to matter and energy a divine spark and presence, based on genuine and proven scientific principals.

But, as noted previously, it is not necessary to adopt this thinking to accept into one's heart and mind the religion offered by the Genuine Hero System. For it is not a religion based on dogma or exclusion, or even faith; but rather, the religion offered by a Genuine Hero System culture depends on commitment to a, most likely, eternal quest for learning the truth about God, a being or existence humans probably can never really grasp or know without becoming gods themselves.

What all the foregoing means is that, at the current level of scientific understanding, the most brilliant among us, do not have a clear or even partial comprehension of the nature of God and the Cosmos. None of the great thinkers down the ages of human history have been able to fathom what God or the Cosmos ultimately are. The Genuine Hero System compels all humans beings to simply admit that at this point in human history and development, we do not know what God is and that it is our destiny and purpose to embark on a journey of discovery.

Chapter Eleven
The Economic System of a
Genuine Hero System

We are all a part of the global society of minds,
and how that society evolves is up to each of us.
          - Eric D. Beinhocker

(A). <u>The Establishment and Evolution of Cultural Economic</u>
<u>Systems</u>

Human cultures adopt and employ various
economic systems for the production and delivery of goods
and services essential for sustaining life and providing for
the general welfare of their constituents. Stated another
way, cultures develop various economic systems that create
wealth – that is, goods and services for the constituents of
the cultures in which they operate.

The economic systems of cultures vary widely in
their wealth creation. Some do it well, others do it poorly.
Human society has always had rich cultures and poor
cultures. Indeed, the study of economics involves, at the
macro level, a review of why some cultures produce a largess

of wealth and others do not.

Of course, the culture offering a Genuine Hero System for the construction of its members' self-esteeming LIEs will likewise require some kind of economic system by which to provide for the basic life sustaining needs of such members and products and services beyond those essential needs. This chapter explores the type of economic system might arise in a culture offering a genuine hero system to its members. A corollary to this question is what economic system is best suited to complement the spiritual and intellectual needs and sensibilities that will arise in a culture offering a Genuine Hero System.

As indicated previously, a Genuine Hero System culture is based upon beliefs in the existence of a God whose true conception is presently unknown to humanity as well as the sanctity of the human species as a creation out of the cosmic goo for some divine and eternal purpose. These beliefs foster methods of actions which enable the individual to fashion an illusion, or ideal LIE, thereby gaining self-esteem in an effort to repress or overcome the death/meaningless anxiety. The economic system which will be spawned and used by individuals residing in a Genuine Hero System culture will thus be engendered or constructed based upon these motivational forces. This Manifesto submits that an economic system will naturally develop in a Genuine Hero System as an evolutionary system that advances the beliefs and goals of such a culture to increase to quality of life for all humans, to enhance the survivability of the human species, and to embark upon a quest for a true comprehension of God and the Cosmos.

Since the publication of Adam Smith's *The Wealth of Nations*, economists have proposed various theories explaining how the economy works in human society. In this effort, they have attempted to devise mathematical models for the operation of markets and the creation of wealth. However, in *The Origin of Wealth: Evolution, Complexity, and the Radical Remaking of Economics,* Harvard economist, Eric Beinhocker, asserts that these historical economic theories fail to describe reality. Instead, he proposes the use of evolutionary theory for determining how economic forces work in society.

According to Beinhocker, evolution is an algorithm or an equation that has application for the develop of systems beyond biological ones. Beinhocker put it this way:

> *Evolution is an algorithm: it is an all-purpose formula for innovation, a formula that, through its special brand of trial and error, creates new designs and solves difficult problems... Evolution creates designs, or more appropriately, discovers designs, through a process of trial and error. A variety of candidate designs are created and tried out in the environment; designs that are successful are retained, replicated, and built upon, while those that are unsuccessful are discarded.*

Beinhocker insists that economic shifts and changes are the result of the process of the evolutionary algorithm of differentiation, selection, and amplification. In this regard, he wrote:

> *Evolution creates designs, or more appropriately, discovers designs, through a process of trial and error. A variety of candidate designs are created and tried out in the environment; designs that are successful are retained, replicated, and built upon, while those that are unsuccessful are discarded.*

Economic systems do not arise in a vacuum. They

are dependent upon, and subservient to, the cultural group from which they arise. Indeed, the cultural economic system is yet another method for self-esteem and LIE construction that motivates behavior dependent upon the hero belief system of the culture in which it arises and operates.

Beinhocker further posits that economic evolution occurs with the combination of three interlinked processes, technological evolution, which involves both the advances of "physical" technologies - the things of inventions, such as rudimentary tools, farming scythes, iron making techniques, internal combustion engines, and the computer – and "social" technologies, which Beinhocker identifies as "settled agriculture, the rule of law, money, joint stock companies, and venture capital." Both technologies are equally important in the economic evolution of a particular culture or group of cultures or the entire human species.

The third process in the evolution or creation of a cultural economic system consists of "business designs", which Beinhocker defines as "encompassing the strategy, organizational structure, management processes, culture, and a host of other factors." According to Beinhocker:

> *Businesses fuse Physical and Social Technologies together and express them into the environment in the form of products and services …[and]…it is the three-way coevolution of Physical Technologies, Social Technologies and business designs that accounts for the patterns of change and growth we see in the economy.*

Finally, Beinhocker asserts:

> *Business designs evolve over time through the process of differentiation, selection, and amplification, with the market*

as the ultimate arbiter of fitness.

In other words, various factors provide the impetus for economic change under the evolutionary algorithm of "differentiation, selection, and amplification." This Manifesto submits that a primary factor fostering and introducing economic change is the hero system of the culture in which an economy arises and operates. The economic system will ultimately become a reflection of the belief system in the culture in which it arises and comes to serve in the process of creating wealth by the production of goods and rendering of services.

The Genuine Hero System offers methods of self-esteem creation based upon beliefs in the sanctity of life in general, and every human life in particular, as well as the species collectively; and, in the existence of a God concept and the relevance of Cosmic purpose. These beliefs will have a dramatic directing or motivating effect on the establishment of new Physical and Social Technologies giving rise to the business designs that determine which goods and services will be produced and distributed to the members of that culture and, equally important, to a determination of the services to be rendered in the culture and given value. The economy of a Genuine Hero System culture will be driven towards creating business designs pursuant to the egalitarian ideal of providing greater wealth to more people, to enhancing the species survivability, and to discovering the truth about God and the Cosmos.

As Beinhocker concluded:

...But we should remember that in evolutionary systems, power comes not from the top down, but from the bottom up. Evolution is a blind process, and the evolutionary algorithm

will respond to whatever fitness function it is given. If, as individual consumers, workers, and voters, we ask the economy and our political institutions to maximize our short term needs, to fill materialistic lives with ever more stuff, and to do so without regard for the health of our planet or the lives of future generations, then that is what we will get.

But there is an alternative. Through the ways in which we spend our money, whom we choose to work for, our votes, and our voices, we can create a fitness function that requires our businesses, governments, and scientific institutions to take a longer-term view and to address the needs of global society in a broader and more sustainable way. If we create such a fitness function, then those institutions and our economy will by necessity adapt and respond to that call.

This Manifesto submits that the adoption of the genuine hero systems by human cultures will created the "fitness function" leading economic systems to change in ways having a positive effect on achieving the goals of such a culture of increasing the quality of life for everyone, advancing the survivability of the human species, and enhancing the quest for the true nature of God and the Cosmos.

(B). The Optimal Economic System of a Genuine Hero System Culture

Whatever the theoretical underpinnings for the development of the economic system in a Genuine Hero System culture, there are essentially three types of such economic systems: capitalist, socialist, and mixed.

Although it is not without its flaws, and as this Manifesto is written in late 2008 and early 2009, seems broken beyond repair, it is submitted that democratic-capitalism is best suited for achieving the goals of increasing the quality of life for everyone in the culture, and for other human beings residing beyond the borders of a particular culture; for enhancing the survivability of the human species; and, for embarking on a quest to determine and comprehend the true nature of God and the Cosmos from which the methods of attaining individual self-esteem and personal immortality for the individual are derived. Capitalism works because it rewards risk-taking, intellect, cleverness, and persistent and consistent striving.

Capitalism is essentially a system facilitating the free and unfettered exchange of goods and services among members of a culture that allows individual creativity and ability to determine the method for such exchange rather than interference in this free market process by that culture system of government. Money – an object of value which in itself has no inherent or direct value, was created at the dawn of human history, to facilitate the exchange of goods and services. In short, the barter system wherein goods and services are exchanged for each other was replaced at some point in the history of the human species by an object representing the relative value of the good or service as determined by the "market" – that is, what other people are willing to pay, as represented by the "money" of that culture, for that good or service. Money is thus the means for exchange of goods and services.

As previously explained, capitalism provides a convenient and quantitative method for self-esteem creation in the individual quest to repress death. If a person is industrious, inventive or clever, he or she can figure out a way to offer a new product or service or produce existing products and services more effectively and efficiently, and thus earn or obtain more money. As noted above, the problem arises when one's drive to accumulate wealth or consumer products or services becomes primary to the individual's LIE. The accumulation of wealth, though immediately rewarding in life, fails to provide a sense of personal immortality. Hence, the old adage, "You can't take it with you." Simply put, death trumps the value of one's bank account.

However, capitalism is still highly constructive in a culture offering a Genuine Hero System by promoting personal striving and achievement in some distinctly measurable way in the pursuit of the culture's goals of enhancing its members quality of life, ensuring the survival of the species, and seeking the true nature of God and the Cosmos. The better the scientist in creating innovative products that help achieve those goals, for instance, the higher his or her income; and, equally important, the more secure and substantial that scientist's self-esteem will become. Thus, his or her ideal LIE repressing the death/ meaninglessness anxiety will become strong and vital.

It has been historically demonstrated that capitalism is the economic system best suited to inspire and achieve the most advanced human civilizations. Conversely, socialism has been shown to be largely unworkable as an economic model. This is due primarily to the failure of planned and collective socialism's use of the economic system to enhance individual self-esteem.

As noted above, the resourceful, diligent and disciplined person will become more successful in achieving societal goals that are deemed valuable and thus worthy of monetary reward. In a Genuine Hero System culture, those goals will involve actions, inventions and innovations that increase the quality of life for others, advance the species prospect for survival, and help the society to gain an better comprehension of God and the Cosmos. Other occupations beyond these that provide ancillary value to the culture by offering pleasant diversions from these primary goals, such as artistic and music entertainers and professional level athletes, will be given appropriately lesser value, but still be given due importance in the formulation of one's self-esteem. However, they will not be given excessive economic value as is evident in the cultures of today.

CHAPTER TWELVE
EPILOGUE: THE GENUINE HERO SYSTEM REVISITED

What is the life enhancing illusion?
- Ernest Becker

So what is the Genuine Hero System?

It is simply a new offering of methods for motivating human behavior enabling the individual to gain a sufficient feeling of self-worth to repress or overcome the stark reality of death. Those methods stem from beliefs that the human species, as a sentient race, is sacredly linked to God in a purposeful universe; that every human life is sacred and must be given dignity; and, that God exists although at this juncture in the spiritual and intellectual development of mankind, the nature of God and His Cosmos is unknown.

Thus, the Genuine Hero System's methods for attaining heroism – that is, self-esteem - stemming from the beliefs underlying such methods, motivate actions that improve the lives of everyone – ourselves and our fellow man, in terms of enhancing health, longevity, intelligence and spirituality, and whatever is needed in the pursuit of what have been termed those "inalienable" rights – life, liberty, and happiness; that enhance the survivability of the human species via scientific research and discovery, and technological progress that moves humanity off to explore the vast and possibly everlasting expanse of outer space; and, that advances a quest of discovering the true nature of God and the Cosmos.

Whatever actions are required to succeed in accomplishing these goals – increasing life quality, enhancing the possibility of humanity's survival, and discovering God – should be given utmost sanction, merit and priority, and be deemed the primary lucrative avenues to self-esteem and personal immortality. They should be deemed important above all other activities. Accordingly, those who succeed in moving the culture toward achievement of these goals should be rewarded and celebrated above all others.

Defining the action methods for attaining heroic defeat of the death/meaningless anxiety, however, is not enough to change humanity from its present lack of clear vision and purpose, and propel it to organize a culture that is equipped to realize its highest potential. First, all men must acknowledge the failure of their present lives to bring them happiness and escape from the fear of death. Second, upon such realization, they must undertake the arduous task of discarding the methods offered by present cultures for constructing self-esteem. In short, they must escape from their life immortality elusions. Finally, they must then embrace the beliefs underlying the Genuine Hero System – the sanctity of life and dignity of human life and the sacredness of the human species as a figment of an existing God - and engage in the action methods for building self-esteem based upon those beliefs.

Only this change of illusion based upon the Genuine

Hero System as the motivational force for humanity will save the species from natural or manmade extinction.

PART THREE

ESTABLISHING GENUINE HERO SYSTEMS AMONG CULTURES

Over the last twenty years, I have come to appreciate an important
meta-idea: that the power of ideas to transform the world is itself
accelerating. Although people readily agree with this observation
when it is simply stated, relatively few observers truly appreciate its
profound implications. Within the next several decades, we will
have the opportunity to apply ideas to conquer age-old problems –
and introduce a few new problems along the way.
- Ray Kurzweil, The Singularity Is Near

Once a metaphysical mutation has arisen, it moves inexorably
towards its logical conclusion. Heedlessly, it sweeps away
economic and political systems, ethical considerations and social
structures. No human agency can halt its progress – nothing, but
another metaphysical mutation.
- Michel Houellebecq, Atomized

CHAPTER THIRTEEN
DISCARDING OLD AND EMBRACING
NEW METHODS OF HEROISM

The emergence and diffusion of Christianity and Islam
was one; the Enlightenment and the ascendancy of science
another. I believe we may be on the verge of a new one.
- George Monbiot, Manifesto For a New World Order

The task of social theory is not to explain guilt away or absorb it
unthinkingly in still another destructive ideology,
but to neutralize it and give it expression in
truly creative and life-enhancing ideologies.
- Ernest Becker

(A). The Need to Discard Old LIEs Constructed From Flawed Cultural Hero Systems

By now the reader should be mulling the idea, if not entirely convinced, that human life is an illusion – or LIE - constructed to overcome the stark reality of death and the related psychological death/meaninglessness anxiety. The illusion itself is constructed from action methods, based upon cultural beliefs, through a programming of the mind in the socialization process by parents, friends, teachers, peers, mass media, and all the other sources of information which communicates, instructs and ultimately programs the human mind as to what is important and real in the world in which we find ourselves living. Unfortunately, those programming instructions are erroneous – what is taught to be real and meaningful are not because in each and every past and present cultural hero system, the reality of death has not, and is not, impressed upon the minds of men and women.

Thus, all present and past beliefs underlying modern and historical cultural hero systems are essentially false or incomplete because such beliefs fail to acknowledge or comprehend that death is the primary reality that motivates human behavior. The failure of past and present cultural hero systems to face up to and acknowledge the stark reality of death as the central motivating force in human life has caused humans to lead what Kierkegaard termed "inauthentic" or "automatic" lives. Such lives are mere symbolic manifestations of a false or inauthentic reality. All existing modern cultural hero systems must therefore be rejected as the basis for the constructing the individual's LIE. Thus, we all must confront the reality of death in the formulation and application of methods for self-esteem creation and connecting to God, and demand that our cultures offer authentic or genuine goals and action methods for doing so.

Kierkegaard recognized that the members of cultures have always been psychologically unhealthy, that they lead "inauthentic" or "automatic" lives. Becker put it this way: "To be a 'normal cultural man,' is for Kierkegaard, to be sick – whether one knows it or not..." To be healthy, Kierkegaard reasoned, man must transcend himself. That is, as this Manifesto postulates and urges, the individual must reject the illusion of his life and the systems of belief and action methods offered by his culture from which it was constructed.

How does one do this – reject one's life as false, inauthentic, unreal and automatic? And what happens once one does so? How does one accept the idea that all one's motivations are built on falsity, error? How does one cope with the stark realization that one's life is built on nothing?

Becker offered this advice:

By realizing the truth of his situation, by dispelling the lie of his character, by breaking his spirit out of its conditioned prison.

Thus, the realization of one in-authenticity is not a bad thing at all, but an escape from one's falsely conditioned prison. The person must break free of the comfort of his illusion that hides from him the reality of death and his animal nature, an illusion constructed from the bricks and mortar of heroic pursuit offered by the false beliefs of culture enabling him to in-authentically and automatically fend off the terror of the human condition. As Becker put it:

In the prison of one's character one can pretend and feel that he is somebody, that the world is manageable, that there is a reason for one's life, a ready justification for one's action. To live automatically and uncritically is to be assured of at least a minimum share of the programmed cultural heroics…

That is – allowing oneself to construct a LIE based upon a modern cultural hero system is to select an easy way to obscure or conceal the reality of death from one's life. One can succeed on some level in that way, even thinking that the life they have led has purpose and meaning. But the truth is certainly otherwise and is lurking at the bottom of one's soul every hour of every day. It is Becker's "worm at the core." Thus, the failure to recognize the deficiency of one's illusion, due to the failure to acknowledge the reality of death, and the failure of one's heroism to provide genuine meaning to one's life, results in an ultimately empty, purposeless, and unhappy life.

Following Kierkegaard's lead, Becker believed that only by escaping from the prison of inauthentic methods for obtaining self-esteem, and their false means to death denial, can the person become an authentic or genuine being ready for a truly meaningful and enduring life experience. The heroism offered by past and present cultures provides only illusory and temporary relief from the anguish of death and meaninglessness. Only when this concept is recognized and acknowledged as an essential truth, can the individual obtain genuine heroism and approach a sincere knowledge of himself, God and the Cosmos.

In short, accepting the reality of death, and one's creatureliness, and thus admitting that one's life is pure fantasy, a mere illusion that has no real meaning beyond one's physical existence, will tend to set one free. Such realization and acceptance will then make the individual ready, willing and able to genuinely resolve the issue of meaning in his or her life.

In his penultimate summary of the awesome truth of Kierkegaard's ideas, Becker put it this way:'

> ...*Man breaks through the bounds of merely cultural heroism; he destroys the character lie that had him perform as a hero in the everyday social scheme of things; and by doing so he opens himself up to infinity, to the possibility of cosmic heroism, to*

the very service of God. His life thereby acquires ultimate value in place of merely social and cultural, historic value. He links his secret inner self, his authentic talent, his deepest feelings of uniqueness, his inner yeaning for absolute significance, to the very ground of creation.

The Genuine Hero System is organized around this principle: that one must break free from the prison of human in-authenticity, admit the falsity of one's character lie (LIE), eschew the easy, blind, automatic life, in which the awareness of death is repressed and forgotten, but never totally, and embrace and confront instead the truth of human creatureliness and the reality of death. Indeed, the Genuine Hero System embraces and revels in the reality of death as a central belief from which methods of action and genuine meaning are offered to individuals in the basic human psychological quest for self-esteem and connection to immortality.

The Genuine Hero System demands that the individual face up to the death/meaningless anxiety, because as Becker realized, only by accepting the truth of the situation one is in – that you are a flesh and blood, defecating creature doomed to die, "can you open a new possibility for yourself." And further: "It is only if you 'taste' death with the lips of your living body that you can know emotionally that you are a creature who will die." Martin Luther put it this way: "I say, die, i.e., taste death as though it were present." [And is this not the real meaning of the Jesus "myth?" Jesus tasted death and returned resurrected, one with God, as God Himself]. Becker added: "What Kierkegaard is saying, in other words, is that the school of anxiety leads to possibility *only by destroying* the vital lie of character."

Thus, for an individual or, preferably, a group of

individuals, to adopt a Genuine Hero System cultural belief system, they must first come to grips with their mortality, accept it as a fact of human life, and then recognize and accept two basic realities: (1). That we are physical creatures who die; and, (2). That there is a supernatural explanation for, and force underlying, the existence of the humanity and the Cosmos (i.e., that there is a God) which we do not yet comprehend.

In short, a Genuine Hero System from which the individual can construct a genuine LIE must be first based upon the recognition of the reality of death rather than in its denial; that God exists in some unknown capacity; and, that the immortality of the soul is actual and present. As Becker summed up it with ever the hint of trepidation:

> *And so the arrival at new possibility, at new reality, by the destruction of the self through facing up to the anxiety of the terror of existence. The self must be destroyed, brought down to nothing, in order for self-transcendence to begin. Then the self can begin to relate itself to powers beyond itself.*

Once such core genuine truths are accepted by the individual (after, no doubt, much self-reflection, debate, self-doubt, and confirmation), he or she can reject the illusion of reality and meaning stemming from his or her present LIE, and fully accept and adopt the methods for self-esteem creation offered by the Genuine Hero System – that is, obtaining self-esteem by engaging in activities that improve the quality of life for all humans; by engaging in activities that enhance the prospect for the eternal survival of the species; and, by pursuing spiritual and intellectual study that increases a comprehension and connection to God and the Cosmos. It is only by doing these things that death can be genuinely overcome, and one's life become authentic, real. It is only by doing this that the individual can attain a grand or ideal illusion and genuinely overcome the terror of death.

In summary, to get from an imperfect and unfulfilling life immortality illusion, built from the beliefs of current cultures, to an ideal illusion constructed from a Genuine Hero System that motivates activities centering around improving one's life, and the lives of other human beings, and in increasing the prospects of the survival of the species, as well as gaining a genuine and more complete understanding of God and the Cosmos, one must do the following:

1. Recognize and accept that one's LIE, or life immortality project, as Becker would call it, is a mere illusion constructed for the express purpose of repressing the death anxiety;

2. Accept that there exists a genuine, supernatural explanation for existence of the Cosmos – that is, there is a God of some kind which we, as individuals and a species, are incapable of comprehending at our present level of cultural, intellectual, spiritual and scientific development;

3. Upon acceptance and recognition of the reality of death and thus the illusory nature of one's life, reject and discard one's present life immortality elusion; and,

4. Become a "genuine hero" or "authentic man" by constructing an "ideal illusion"

using the action methods offered by the Genuine Hero System, which themselves stem from beliefs in the reality of death and of the existence of God, and in the sanctity of the individual human life and of humanity, to satisfy the urge toward attaining individual self-esteem and a connection to an immortal beyond in order to repress or overcome the death/meaninglessness anxiety in an ideal or complete way.

To state it yet again, the Genuine Hero System, being based on the reality of death, and the existence of some kind of yet-to-be-humanly-comprehended God and Cosmos, as well as the sacredness of humanity, offers the individual with genuine methods for overcoming the death/meaninglessness anxiety – by attacking it head on by the pursuit of activities which increase the quality of life for everyone, and which enhance humanity's ability to survive as a species. Performing these acts upon the belief that the evolutionary "creation" and survival of Mankind is of primary importance and meaning, will provide human beings with the necessary ingredients for self-esteem construction capable of overcoming the death/meaninglessness anxiety that will enable them to live genuinely meaningful, happy and fulfilled lives. In addition, the Genuine Hero System offers a true religion which not only acknowledges the existence of God, but also accepts our lack of comprehension of just what God is, and then mandates that the species faithfully embark on a heroic and perhaps eternal quest to seek that comprehension upon the sincere hope that it can and will be attained.

Only when the person casts aside one's debilitating and limiting life illusion built from his or her present cultural hero system, and becomes a "genuine hero," living the ideal illusion, will the pursuit of true happiness and individual fulfillment be possible.

Of course, proscribing a general set of actions for improving human existence, and enabling the species to reach its full potential, is one thing, and getting the patient to take the medication for obtaining that result is another. The remainder of this chapter suggests ways in which that may be accomplished. This Manifesto, of course, is a necessary first step of spreading the message and convincing others of its truth.

(B). Constructing A New, Ideal LIE

Becker recognized the difficulty of getting humans to acknowledge and accept that the goals to which they aspire, and the things that they do, stemming from the motivational forces in their lives, are the product of mere illusion, constructed from symbolic methods for obtaining heroism enabling them to deny or repress the underlying fear of death that haunts their lives. Indeed, he wrote:

...to become conscious of what one is doing to earn his feeling of heroism is the main self-analytical problem of life..

If we were to peel away this massive disguise, the blocks of repression over human techniques for earning glory, we would arrive at the potentially most liberating question of all, the main problem of human life: How especially true is the cultural hero system that sustains and drives one?

Stated another way, to succeed in developing a new way of life needed to secure mankind's survival and avoidance of Becker's prognosis of doom, human beings must become aware that one's life is a mere construct, an illusion, and that such illusion must be cast aside since it is founded and built on a false conception of reality. Once liberated from these illusions, humans can begin to embark on a new way to glory, or self-esteem, that not only inspires individual happiness, but can be parlayed into the general good and the potential salvation for humanity.

But Becker was only partially right in his assertion that the main psychological problem the individual must wrestle with is the LIE he has constructed from the hero system in the culture in which he or she reside. The problem for human psychological health is not only in acknowledging the illusion of one's life as a quest for heroism in the denial of reality, but also in thwarting the distress such recognition will necessarily entail by finding and accepting a substitute or replacement vehicle for heroism as the motivational force in one's life. The trick is thus to construct one's life immortality project, one's LIE, as we have termed it, from a new system of thought and belief, replacing what cultures have hither-to-fore offered for doing so, that is based upon a kind of primitive "genuine" heroism which benefits the person individually while collectively advancing the species and enhancing its survivability.

This Manifesto has described the Genuine Hero System in previous chapters as a modern form of primitive heroism which prizes the individual's contribution to improving, advancing and insuring the quality of life for all humans, and to enhancing the species' opportunity for eternal survival, as well as embarking on a long-term if not eternal quest for a comprehension of the nature of God and the Cosmos through scientific study and spiritual and intellectual contemplation.

The next chapter of this Manifesto attempts to provide a blueprint for convincing and assisting human beings of the absolute and unwavering need to acknowledge the falsity of their present LIEs in the process of renouncing them, and to adopt the motivational force in their lives based upon genuine heroism.

CHAPTER FOURTEEN
IMPLEMENTATION OF THE GENUINE HERO SYSTEM:
SPREADING THE MESSAGE

*There is nothing more powerful than
an idea whose time has come.*
- Victor Hugo

(A). <u>Cultural Evolution: Survival of the Fittest</u>

Social anthropologists and sociologists have long theorized that human cultures engage in a kind of evolution similar to biological evolution. Indeed, Charles Darwin borrowed the phrase, "survival of the fittest" from the English sociologist, Edward Spencer, who had used it in explaining how cultures progress and change.

As noted by Rodney Stark in his 2007 book, *Discovering God*: "Theories of the evolution of human culture must differ substantially from theories of biological evolution, since culture has no equivalent to genes, and is not transmitted in a "mechanical" way, but only imperfectly through the socialization of the young." Stark goes on to state: "However, both biological and cultural evolution seem to be greatly shaped by the principle of *natural selection* or *survival of the fittest.*"

While this position ignores the possibility of the evolution of culture through the radical spread of new and transforming ideas, known as "memes" or Ideaviruses, discussed later in this Manifesto, it nevertheless raises the compelling prospect that the human culture adopting a Genuine Hero System as the motivating force for its members could become the fittest and dominate one among human cultures and thus replace or subsume existing cultures into its bosom. This assumes, of course, that this Manifesto is correct in its forecast that a Genuine Hero System will motivate great advances in those human cultures in which it is adopted, and thus outstrip other contemporary cultures which do not, and thus come to represent the next step in human cultural evolution.

In support of this very point, Stark further points out:

> *As proposed by Spencer, the principle of the survival of the fittest meant that, within particular circumstances, those cultures and/or cultural elements better suited to human needs will survive and those less suited will tend to die out. This may occur because a society shifts its cultural elements accordingly,* **or because the society itself (and its culture) succumbs to another having a better-suited culture.** (emphasis added)

Stark noted that he "fundamental mechanisms" of human cultural evolution "are human creativity and evaluation....Hence:

> *Humans will tend to adopt and retain those elements of culture that appear to produce 'better' results, while those that appear*

to be less rewarding will tend to be discarded."

This Manifesto submits that individuals who adopt methods for obtaining self-esteem from among those offered by a Genuine Hero System will conduct themselves in ways that advance human spiritual, intellectual and technological achievement, as well as individually attaining a higher level of happiness and fulfillment, since they will be better adjusted to the death/meaninglessness anxiety than their non-Genuine Hero System brethren. Thus, Genuine Hero System dominated cultures will advance beyond other cultures through the strength of character, confidence, general mental stability and happiness, science, spirituality, knowledge and invention of their members. In short, because a better adjusted, more fulfilled, mentally and emotional stable, complete and happy populace will be produced in Genuine Hero System cultures, such cultures will naturally outpace and ultimately dominate non-Genuine Hero System cultures.

Thus, the Genuine Hero System cultures will eventually become the controlling human cultures on earth because they will engender better peoples and superior spiritual, intellectual and technological advances. At some point in the process of this transformation, Genuine Hero System cultures will ultimately join together to form one conglomerate or confederated global Genuine Hero System culture seeking the advances for all humanity that have already been achieved in individual cultural groups that have adopted the Genuine Hero System approach to self-esteem/ LIE creation. It is at this point when humanity will finally start to achieve its promised greatness, resulting in a true utopian golden age which mankind has envisioned since the dawn of history.

(B). The Power of "Memes" and "Ideaviruses" To Change Cultures

As this Manifesto has firmly argued, unless human cultures adopt new hero systems, and indeed the Genuine Hero System, for motivating the conduct of their members, and ultimately becomes unified under a single government employing a singular Genuine Hero System for the construction of the life immortality elusions by their citizens, the species is doomed to ultimate extinction either by manmade or natural cataclysm.

To avoid the extinction, this Manifesto demands that humans acknowledge the fallacy and insufficiency of the hero systems in the culture in which they reside, and reject and discard them in constructing their life immortality elusions – that semblance of personal existence which symbolically denies the reality of death and motivates thought and conduct. Humans must accept the methods for self-esteem creation offered by a Genuine Hero System that are based upon beliefs that the survival of mankind, and the enhancement of the quality and quantity of human life, are of primary importance; and, that one's pursuit of self-esteem should be satisfied by actions which advance those beliefs or goals. The Genuine Hero System is thus based on the pursuit of such goals which advance the quality and length of individual and collective human life, as well as the survival of the species. It is, in large measure both a religious and political ideology based upon one's acceptance of the sanctity of the individual human, the human species, and the species' rightful and consequent quest for a genuine understanding of Nature and God.

A culture offering the Genuine Hero System as its motivational force also requires its constituents to acknowledge that while there is a supernatural aspect to being and life, the present comprehension of God and the Cosmos is vastly incomplete. Heroism is satisfied in such a culture by pursuing spiritual and intellectual activities that advance the quest for such comprehension.

The next question, then, is how does one achieve the seemingly herculean, if not impossible, task of convincing the individual and whole human societies to reject and discard the present deficient hero systems to construct LIEs that ultimately fail the individual in his or her need to repress the death/meaninglessness anxiety, and the species in gaining eternal salvation, to cultures which embrace and employ the Genuine Hero System to motivate their constituents? How does one move so many individuals seemingly trapped by their present illusions of meaning to acknowledge the fallacy and impotence of such illusions in overcoming the fear of death that causes them, ultimately, to become unhappy and unfulfilled?

The concept of *memes* or "idea-viruses" may be the marketing tool needed for spreading this Manifesto's message of radical change in the way individuals construct their life immortality elusions and attain a sense of self-esteem by embracing the methods for doing so offered by the Genuine Hero System. Indeed, memes may be the key to human salvation so that humanity may avoid extinction and escape from its present state of stunted progress.

So what are *memes* or idea-viruses? And how can they be spread through a culture, indeed, throughout the entire human race?

The word, "meme," was coined in 1976 by zoologist and evolutionary scientist, Richard Dawkins, in his book, *The Selfish Gene.* (This is the same author who wrote the atheistic leaning, *The God Delusion,* discussed earlier) Dawkins based its invention and use on the Greek word, "*mimeme,*" which essentially means, something imitated. It refers to an idea, or unit of information, transferable from one mind to another. Examples of memes, according to Dawkins, are tunes, quotes, fashions, fads, or beliefs.

A meme has been characterized as a kind of idea virus or thought gene that replicates itself, and evolves, as it is transferred and processed from person to person and group to group. *Memeplexes* are cooperative sets of memes which coalesce and become integrated within a culture, such as religious beliefs or political ideologies.

Under this theory, the Christian memeplexe evolved from Jewish religious teachings, as altered or evolved first, according to historical fashion, by Jesus, and as later interpreted and refined by Paul of Tarsus. Christianity further evolved to form ultimately, the complex coda of beliefs and dogma of the Roman Catholic church. The schism between the Roman Catholic and Eastern Orthodox churches, and later splits in Catholicism giving rise to the Protestant reformation, was the result of groups within the Christian sect adding new, or modifying existing individual memes, in the ever-evolving *memeplex* that had started out simply as Christianity – a belief in the message, and later, the divinity of Jesus Christ..

The concept of memes was given a popular spin by Malcolm Gladwell's 2000 best-seller, *The Tipping Point,* in which Gladwell explained how new cultural ideas or fads, services or products spread and become widely and wildly popular once they "tip." Gladwell's theory described how ideas that start off small and sometimes innocuously, perhaps emanating from the mind of a single person, or small group of persons, are imparted to others and become culturally popular "social epidemics." Once these ideas, or memes, "tip," they become popular ideological phenomenon.

Gladwell suggested that the waves of change that sometimes overcome a culture, and alter the way its members behave and think, are like sicknesses, and the vehicles for such change are thought viruses, the "memes" referred to by Dawkins. Gladwell summarized his theory this way:

> *It is that the best way to understand the emergence of fashion trends, the ebb and flow of crime waves, or, for that matter, the transformation of unknown books into bestsellers, or the rise of teenage smoking, or the phenomena of the word of mouth, or any number of the other mysterious changes that mark everyday life is to think of them as epidemics. Ideas and products and behaviors spread just like viruses do.*

Gladwell cited as an example for his theory the hush-puppie shoe craze in the late 1980s. He also pointed to other fads, that spread from modest, almost imperceptible beginnings, to become major marketing successes.

The question, of course, is how this occurs, and how the theory of social epidemics via an idea-virus, or "meme," can be applied to spreading the ideas underlying this Manifesto to a wider population in order to enhance its implementation among all human cultures.

In *Unleashing the Ideavirus,* Seth Godin took this idea a step further by arguing that traditional marketing techniques, which he termed "interruption marketing," such as television commercials, may no longer be effective, and cost-effective, in spreading revolutionary transforming social and marketing trends. Rather, he surmised that "the future belongs to marketers who establish a foundation and process where interested people can market to *each other.*"

For Godin, marketing must become a process where consumer networks are ignited and work on their own to spread an idea, service or product. Instead of marketing at people with, for instance, a barrage of annoying and costly television commercials, he proposed that the public can be sold on an idea simply by putting into motion effective word-of-mouth or other consumer-to-consumer mechanisms. Godin puts it this way:

> The holy grail for anyone who traffics in ideas is this: to unleash an ideavirus…An idea that just sits there is worthless. But an idea that moves and grows and infects everyone it touches… that's an ideavirus.

So how does one unleash the idea-virus or memes that will implement the ideas and message of this Manifesto in achieving its quest for human advancement, salvation and happiness? Can such drastic and irrevocable change to human society be realized by mere word-to-mouth transmission or an internet campaign? In short, what steps are necessary to get to the ideas of this manifesto to and beyond the tipping point?

In *The Tipping Point,* Gladwell theorized that social epidemics are first and foremost the product of "mavens," those individuals who accumulate knowledge and craft a new way of thought or theory, a virus or meme sought to be spread until it becomes the social epidemic. As Gladwell put it: "To be a maven is to be a teacher….Mavens are really information brokers, sharing and trading what they know… In a social epidemic….mavens provide the message." Jesus Christ, St. Paul, Karl Marx, Darwin, Ernest Becker, and this writer, for that matter, are as examples of mavens.

But for a social epidemic to effectively and successfully be spread to reach the maximum numbers of individuals that will result in a dramatic change in the culture, mavens need those individuals Gladwell termed, "connectors," the "select group of people...with the skills to persuade," and "salesmen" (whom, for his part, Godin termed, "sneezers"), those individuals with the often uncanny ability of convincing others of the efficacy of the Maven's message or idea who might not otherwise be impressed with it. Gladwell summed it up this way:

> *Mavens are data banks. They provide the message. Connectors are the social glue: they spread it. But there is also a select group of people – Salesmen – with the skills to persuade us when we are unconvinced of what we are hearing, and they are as critical to the tipping of word-of-mouth epidemics as the other two groups.*

Godin argued that important ideas are essentially like atoms making up a molecule. He termed such series of connected ideas fittingly, as a *"manifesto,"* as those ideas are expressed and coordinated in this Manifesto, "a powerful, logical 'essay' that assembles a bunch of existing ideas and creates a new one." He goes on to state that a *manifesto* can be a book, like this one, or an image, a song, a product or process.

Whatever the medium or format (book, music, etc.) used by the *manifesto* to impart itself to an audience is of no matter – what matters is the message. Godin stated: "As long as you can use your manifesto to change the way people think, talk or act...you can create value." Thus, an idea-virus is "a big idea that runs amok across the target audience."

What Godin and Gladwell thus share is the belief that if the manifesto, idea, essay or meme is compelling enough, it can be effectively spread by word-of-mouth, person to person, whether, as Gladwell suggested, by connectors or salesmen (or Godin's "sneezers"), or by the readers of this Manifesto. In short, a Madison Avenue marketing blitz is no longer necessary in the present world of global, internet communication, to spread a brilliantly and convincingly stated, life-altering message that can ultimately have an impact upon collective human behavior. And assuming the idea is compelling enough, once the flow of information starts, the spread of the idea has a chance to become a tidal wave, or "tipping point," immersing and flooding the culture into a cataclysm of meaningful and permanent social change.

Godin also suggested that idea-viruses can be spread easier and more cheaply than ever before. There are simply more avenues of communication available to do so – the so-called information revolution sparked by the explosion of television networks, radio stations, self-publishing, and of course, the internet, provides an idea maven, and his connectors and salesmen and sneezers, with ample means by which to spread the message.

In sum, for the ideas or "manifesto," using Godin's terminology, of this book to become a dramatic epidemic of meaningful social change, it must first and foremost communicate a comprehensible and compelling revolutionary message. Assuming that it does, then the tools available among human cultures must be identified and put to work in spreading the message of this Manifesto beyond Gladwell's tipping point.

While the ideas underlying this Manifesto, calling as it does for individuals to reject and discard their present lifestyles and with them, their socio-economic, religious, political, and national beliefs and allegiances, in favor of one that demands and compels duty to one's fellow man, one's species, and one's God via a quest for comprehending

His true state, are necessarily radical and will seem to some, out-of-the-box fantastic, or even downright crazy, they are unique and interesting enough to merit notice and scrutiny and perhaps, acceptance. Therefore, they are the type of "idea-viruses" Godin and Gladwell believe are ripe for spreading to the members of cultures by the new and formidable marketing techniques which have become available to so many in this revolutionary age of instant, global information and communication.

However, to be successful in actually implementing the ideas of this manifesto, other human beings must be convinced that such ideas are valid – that one's life is really an illusion, constructed from methods offered by the cultures to enable the individual to overcome the death/meaninglessness anxiety; and, that the methods offered by past and present cultures to fashion such illusion have motivated human beings to conduct themselves in ways that are trivial or inimical to the achieving mankind's highest spiritual, intellectual and technological potential.

Assuming that these radical ideas are compelling enough, the next and equally important step will be to devise the means to spread them to the masses in the hope that the mythical tipping point posited by Gladwell can be reached and surpassed. The marketing tools suggested by Godin and Gladwell, via word of mouth, seem best suited to maximize the potential for spreading the message of this Manifesto since it is unlikely that traditional marketing vehicles will have the desire effect of convincing individuals to give up their cultural LIEs.

(C). The Role of Education In Spreading the Idea of the GHS

One of the by-products of past and present cultural hero systems is the failure of the human education process.

Human cultures are sorely lacking in their ability to adequately educate their members. A major reason for this, of course, is that so little financial and intellectual resources are invested among cultures on the development and advancement of their education systems. Such resources are wasted on trivial or wasteful pursuits spawned by the cultural hero systems. The result is millions upon millions of ignorant and impoverished human beings and wasted, useless and purposeless lives.

The large number of uneducated or under-educated persons alive today is perhaps the greatest impediment to the establishment and spread of the Genuine Hero System among present cultural groups, and will ultimately hold back the unification of the human species under a single cultural and governmental system. An educated person whose understanding of the reality of the world has been expanded by knowledge and truth in a properly functioning education system will not be prone to adopting false or mythical religious beliefs, and will recognize that various other pursuits, such as sports spectator-ism or celebrity worship, are mere trivial diversions which should not distract the person and the species from the larger and more meaningful purposes of improving individual lives, increasing the species' survival potential, and seeking the true spiritual nature of God.

Furthermore, a properly and fully educated person will be able to recognize the reality of death, raise the veil of his or her life illusion, and see clearly what the purpose of life should be – to overcome the stark reality of death through belief in the sanctity of mankind and the existence of God. Increasing the education level of humans will have the effect of giving the ideavirus of this Manifesto the medium by which it can be effectively spread.

As will be further detailed below, the creation of an

educational institution, *The Foundation For Human Salvation*, whose mission will be to advance the ideas of this Manifesto, will be one significant way, among others, to educate humanity as to the reality of death, the need to acknowledge that reality and reject the present life immortality illusions, or projects, offered by today's cultures, and to construct an ideal life illusion motivating actions that improve the lives of others, enhance the survivability of the human species, and seek the truth about God and the Cosmos.

Only by announcing the truth about reality in the vast array of communication media available to modern man, and by using all available educational resources, including a foundation whose singular purpose is to inoculate the *meme* or idea-virus of this Manifesto, can the Genuine Hero System become the sole means for offering methods to self-esteem and LIE construction for the cultures and peoples of the world.

(D). Epilogue: The Socialization of Genuine Heroism

The use of memes or Ideaviruses, and education, especially through The Foundation for Human Survival, to spread the word about the need to discard the present hero systems offered by cultures to construct LIEs and to replace them with the Genuine Hero System methods to self-identity and human advancement, is really an aspect of altering the socialization process for the fashioning of human character. This is because the socialization process is at the heart of that fashioning. Humans are programmed to action by the beliefs offered by the cultures in which they reside because those beliefs are the motivating forces in society. They believe because they are programmed to believe.

Therefore, the only way for the individual "program" to be changed from the present one, which fails to produce humans capable of genuine happiness and fulfillment, and of establishing social groups that ensure a good or dignified quality of life for all humans, not to mention the survival of the group, is to spread the message of this Manifesto to the maximum number of individuals. From the outset of their discovery and comprehension of the world, children must be "inoculated" with the beliefs underlying the Genuine Hero System by parents, schools and the media. That is, they must be brought up on the firm belief in the sanctity of the individual, in the sacred role of the human animal in cosmic evolution, and in the existence of a God that has some as o f yet unknown role and purpose in the Cosmic drama.

Until the message of this Manifesto takes hold and spreads via the concept of memes or by whatever force it occurs, engendering the beginning and continuation of the Genuine Hero System socialization process, mankind will continue to wallow in cultures wrongfully prizing the destructive and the trivial and producing unhappy constituents.

CHAPTER FIFTEEN
THE FEDERALIST MODEL FOR A
WORLD GENUINE HERO SYSTEM

The new mutation will force us to abandon nationhood, just as, in earlier epochs, we abandoned barony and the clan. It will compel us to recognize the irrationalities that set us apart. For the first time in history, we will see ourselves as a species.
- George Monbiot

(A). <u>Introduction: Discarding and Replacing of Existing Cultural Hero Systems</u>

      This Manifesto aims to convince humanity that in order to achieve individual happiness and collective peace and prosperity, not to mention the survival of the human species, the old ways employed by human beings to organize and govern themselves must be discarded. Hero systems define the style of political organizations that arise among cultures. They go hand in hand and, in fact, the political system is another method of attaining self-esteem and constructing the member's LIE.

      Humans must transform the respective hero system in the culture in which they reside into a Genuine

Hero System for attaining self-esteem that will motivate them to actions promoting and improving the quality of life for themselves and their fellow humans, as well as collectively enhancing the prospect of human survival and an opportunity of comprehending the nature of God and the Cosmos. Furthermore, to attain an utopian society that can best offer the human species a realistic hope of eternal, evolutionary survival, a unified or singular type of culture, offering methods for obtaining self-esteem to its members under a more or less uniform Genuine Hero System of belief, must evolve among the existing and often competing cultures and be joined into a common human cultural group under a global human government.

Therefore, the Genuine Hero System proposed by this Manifesto also necessarily envisions a new method of government based upon its underlying principles. The guiding principles of a government borne from a culture offering a Genuine Hero System include promulgating and effectuating policies that increase the quality of life for all members of the group being governed; legislating actions which enhance the survivability of the species; and, providing an environment of absolute religious tolerance that advances the quest to find the true nature of God.

In sum, to achieve the ideal human society, this Manifesto insists that human cultures must adopt the beliefs underlying a Genuine Hero System. However, it is not necessary, at least initially, for such cultures to immediately become part of a single, unified world government. Indeed, to propose such immediate option as a plan to save humanity would be unrealistic and indeed, undesirable. Rather the formation of independent genuine hero system states, each offering their unique brand of methods for attaining genuine heroism for their respective constituents, will initially best serve the spiritual and intellectual development of the human species.

However, humanity cannot get to that point under the present, anachronistic, out-moded style of governance. It is obvious that the international bodies such as the United Nations does not have the weight of authority to prevent humans from engaging in cataclysmic wars or other acts of destruction and wasteful use of mental, physical and financial resources and energy. Therefore, as soon as possible, this Manifesto urges humanity to form a loosely centralized government based upon the principles of federalism. To do otherwise is to invite, as we have seen, eventual war among peoples, and the scattering and diffusion of human spiritual, intellectual, technological and financial resources.

The trick, of course, is finding the way to get from the point of discord which currently marks the diverse cultures of humanity, and their respective hero systems, to the point of relative commonality of heroism and government among the human family. Toward that lofty end, this Manifesto proposes that the political concept of *federalism*, as used with relative success as an organizing and governing principle by the colonial Americans of the Revolutionary War era in ultimately establishing the United States of America in 1789, be employed as the model for establishing a bold, new world order compelling wildly diverse human groups to join into a unified federation of national sovereign cultures in offering common methods under the Genuine Hero System for obtaining death denying self-esteem and heroism for its respective peoples that will contribute, rather than stunt and stifle, world prosperity, individual happiness, and foster the hope of eternal human survival.

The transformation from modern, diverse cultural blueprints for heroism under the present world system, to a global Genuine Hero System culture, must practically speaking, necessarily be a gradual one in light of the long history of separate cultural nationalities and the certain jealousies that will remain among them, much like existed among the original thirteen colonies of the United States both before, and after, ratification of the Constitution. It must also be a gradual one so as to insure that no despots or psychotic predatory groups attempt to take control and dictate the composition of the culture's hero system and, through the socialization process and otherwise, the methods offered by the society for the construction of its members' LIEs. Plus, as noted previously, having several cultures experiment with the appropriate methods for gaining self-esteem using a Genuine Hero System will actually be beneficial in devising a common plan applicable to the most benefit for all humanity in some future epoch.

The concept of federalism is perhaps the only principle for inter-governmental and cultural organization existing for persuading humanity to become unified under a common Genuine Hero System in a gradual yet definitive and reasonably orderly way. Presently, humanity is divided into numerous cultural groups, known as sovereign nations, consisting of varying populations residing within, and separated from each other, by usually carefully and clearly defined geographic boundaries. Each of these human groups/units/nations are comprised of a roughly homogenous individuals who possess common religious, political and socio-economic beliefs. Based upon these beliefs, through the socialization process of familial, educational and environmental upbringing and indoctrination, the citizens of these nations come to believe in, and use, the methods offered by the national cultural hero system to construct their individual LIEs and then act accordingly in their everyday lives; and, by gaining understanding and faith in these beliefs, constructing their LIEs, and taking actions in conformance therewith, they are able to gain a measure of self-esteem and connection to some supernatural Beyond – or God concept, which *in toto* enables them to overcome or repress the death/meaninglessness anxiety.

Similar types of cultural hero systems are common to many nations since so much of human hero systems are dependent upon religious belief. For example, the Arabian nations – such as Saudi Arabia, Kuwait, Iraq, Palestine, Syria, Egypt, Libya and Iran – have developed rather similar methods for constructing individual LIEs for attaining self-esteem since their culture hero systems are each based upon the religious belief of Islam. Likewise, Christianity has fostered common cultural hero systems in the civilizations of Western Europe and the post-Columbian Americas. A third major grouping of nations in the Far East – including China, India, and Japan – are connected by the common ideals expressed in the eastern philosophies of Buddhism, Hinduism, Confucianism, and Taoism, among others.

As this Manifesto has expressed, the hero systems which have developed under each of these major groupings of national cultures have been woefully deficient in motivating harmonious and progressive human action that benefits the individual and collective good. Indeed, history demonstrates quite the contrary - that the heroism fomented by each of the Arabian, Western and Eastern national cultural groupings and their sub-groupings has led to destructive or inconsequential pursuits, and as amply demonstrated by the current state of human affairs, has utterly failed to enable mankind to reach its highest spiritual, intellectual or technological potential.

The pursuit of individual and group heroism

to date, inspired by the past and present cultural hero systems, represents an embarrassing failure of human accomplishment and intellect. The tragedy is that this failure is not due to some inherent defect of the human intellect or even character. Instead, it is solely attributable to the shortcomings of the methods offered by human cultures to avoid the tension and terror of the reality of life and death. The further message of this Manifesto is that there exists a set of motivational forces, based upon methods for self-esteem construction offered by the Genuine Hero Belief System, that are capable of inspiring and directing human beings to action that benefits themselves, other humans, the human species as a whole and that enables them to gain a true comprehension of God and the Cosmos.

A change in beliefs underlying the existing cultural hero systems, which have arisen and developed over many thousands of years of indoctrination of human populations large and small, is of course an enormous and revolutionary undertaking. Rather than advocating violent revolution to effect such change, this Manifesto proposes that the concept of Federalism be put to full and effective use as the means for promoting the gradual change from the hero systems offered by the present national cultural groupings, and their sub-groupings, to the implementation of the Genuine Hero Systems in each of them.

Of course, it is the ultimate hope of this Manifesto that federalism will lead to a common version of the General Hero System under a more or less centralized world government that takes collective action to enhance the quality of life and pursuit of happiness for each of its citizens, ensure the survival of the human species, and seek the true nature of God and the Cosmos through scientific study and spiritual enlightenment.

(B). <u>Federalism</u>

What is *federalism*? And how can it be used to peacefully form a world government of nations organized under the principle of genuine heroism?

In <u>Theories of Federalism: A Reader</u>, Dimitrios Karmis and Wayne Norman offer the following definition:

> *In its most general sense, federalism is an arrangement in which two or more self-governing communities share the same political space. Citizens of federal states ... are members of both their subunit...and the larger federation as a whole.*

According to Alexander Hamilton, John Jay, and James Madison, in <u>The Federalist Papers</u>, the Constitution of the United States is "federalist" in its foundation because its ratification:

> *...is to be given by the people, not as individuals comprising one entire nation, but as comprising the distinct and independent States to which they respectively belong...Each State, in ratifying the Constitution, is considered a sovereign body, independent of all others, and only to be bound by its voluntary act.*
>
> - *See,* Federalist 39

They go on to state that the constitution creates a national government in the sense that the powers of that government operate "on the individual citizens composing the nation" rather than "the political borders composing the confederacy."

The existing national cultural groupings should unite under a similar federalist constitutional structure in which they would retain their independence and identity

– that is, their sovereignty - while joining with the other nations to engage in mutually beneficial actions to improve the quality of life for peoples residing in individual States, while working to prevent warfare and discord between nations, and pursing policies that advance the survivability of the species and quest for God.

Federalism on a regional scale has already been employed among many nations with diverse backgrounds and cultural beliefs with evident success. In addition to the United States of America, a early example of federalism is the city-state confederacy of ancient Greece. As noted in by Alexander Hamilton and James Madison in *The Federalist Papers, No. 18:*

> *Among the confederacies of antiquity the most considerable was the Grecian republics…*[bearing]*…a very instructive analogy to the present Confederation of the American States. The members retained the character of independent and sovereign states and had equal votes in the federal council.*

Of more recent vintage, the European Union, a product of various political and economic treaties spanning several decades, was formally established in 1993 by the Treaty of Maastricht and is a modern example of a hybrid form of a federalist government formed among nation-states which have disparate and often conflicting histories, language and economic interests. The Union currently comprises 27 member nations spanning the continent of Europe, including Great Britain, France, Germany, and Italy, which within the last century were at war with each other. Though largely a product of intergovernmentalism, it has established various agencies, so-called supranational bodies, which make decisions binding on all members. Important institutions that have arisen under the Union include a European Parliament, Court of Justice, and Central Bank, all features of a federalist state. The Union operates under a single economic market and certain of the member states have adopted a uniform currency, the *euro*. Thus, the European Union illustrates that diverse nations, with varying socio-economic, political and religious backgrounds, can come together for the common good.

However, it is not fatal to the hoped for worldwide implementation of the Genuine Hero System if it is initially limited to singular cultural groups until it spreads regionally and at last, globally. As the principles of the Genuine Hero System improve the lives of members of individual cultures adopting it as the motivational force for their respective citizenry, and causes them to advance spiritually, intellectually, and technologically above and beyond those other nations still employing the old methods for attaining heroism and self-esteem, it will undoubtedly become adopted by more and more nations and their citizens. Ultimately, at some point in the future, genuine heroism will becomes a global institution of a worldwide human confederacy dedicated to the pursuit of activities that advance individual plenty and freedom, enhance the survivability of the species, and progress the quest for the comprehension of the true God.

Chapter Sixteen
Spreading the Message: The Foundation For Human Survival

These twelve Jesus sent out, instructing them, "Go nowhere among the Gentiles and enter no town of the Samaritans, but go rather to the lost sheep of the house of Israel. And proclaim as you go, saying, 'The kingdom of heaven is at hand.'
- Matthew 10:5-7

And Jesus came and said to them, "All authority in heaven and on earth has been given to me. Go therefore and make disciples of all nations, baptizing them in the name of the Father and of the Son and of the Holy Spirit, teaching them to observe all that I have commanded you. And behold, I am with you always, to the end of the age."
- Matthew 28:18-20

In and what you have heard from me in the presence of many witnesses entrust to faithful men who will be able to teach others also.
- Timothy 2:2

I must proclaim the good news of the kingdom of God
to the other cities also; for I was sent for this purpose.
- Luke 4:43

If humanity is to have any chance of adopting the principles of this Manifesto, and avoiding the doom that Ernest Becker feared otherwise awaits it, there must be undertaken a concerted and vigorous effort to spread its message – with evangelistic zeal and determination - by what hopefully will become an army of committed and excited disciples who have come to adopt its philosophy and message.

As Jesus instructed his disciplines and many followers (assuming one believes that Jesus existed) to spread his essential and primary message that the reign and authority of God was at hand, those who are committed to the prescriptions of this book, calling for the implementation of Genuine Hero Systems as the motivating force for human conduct in all cultures, cannot sit idly back and await some magical change in the methods from which life illusions for death denial which currently motivate human action are constructed. Rather, they must actively take part in convincing others, through their individual and collective words and deeds, to embrace a grand, ideal life illusion constructed from methods of attaining self-esteem and a personal connection with immortality offered by a Genuine Hero System that seeks to increase the quality of life for others, enhance the survivability of the human species, and embark on a quest of discovery of the true nature of God and the Cosmos. They must become the salesman and connectors, as Gladwell suggested, or the sneezers, as Godin termed them, infecting others with the idea-virus of radical change proffered by this Manifesto.

Toward that the achievement of such evangelical

purpose, in tandem with the publication of this Manifesto, a non-profit organization, "The Foundation For Human Survival," is in the process of being established, organized and put into action. The mission of this Foundation is to communicate the message of this book to all those who might listen, to the widest possible audience, in ways that are understandable and reflective of its theoretical underpinnings.

Thus, individuals with a talent for such communication must be immediately recruited to assist in the effort of educating all humanity, reaching out to everyone who might listen, the educated and un-educated alike. No matter the educational level, or intelligence of the individual, the socialization process of the present cultural hero systems have programmed human beings, for the most part, into living false and empty illusions. Thus, most men are oblivious to the realities of life, unaware as to what is truly important in the effort to gain self-esteem and happiness, not to mention a connection with God and the Cosmos and thus the promise of personal immortality. Moreover, they are unaware that under the present illusions motivating their actions, they are often acting at odds with advancing the quality of life for themselves and their fellow man as well as the survivability of the human species. Certainly, they are no closer to a true vision or comprehension of God than their ancestors who reached out for such comprehension from the dawn of human evolution.

Therefore, the disciples of this Manifesto must be committed to communicating its message with a zeal and fervor suitable to overcome the false illusions of the great majority of mankind programmed by the socialization process for countless centuries. They will surely be scoffed at, if not themselves harshly or cruelly prosecuted for preaching to the masses of men the dour truth that the lives they have been leading are false, that they are built from false or incompetent systems of belief, and that they must therefore reject and discard such illusions and build new ones based upon the quest for genuine heroism proposed by this Manifesto. It will not be easy to convince a man that his life is false and that truth lies elsewhere. The message of this Manifesto must be spread in order to help avoid the doom which Becker feared would be the destiny of mankind if he did not face up to his condition.

CHAPTER SEVENTEEN
A POSSIBLE UTOPIA: LIFE UNDER
A GENUINE HERO SYSTEM

The gauge of a truly free society would be the extent to which it admitted its own central fear of death and questioned its own system of heroic transcendence – and that is what democracy is doing most of the time.
- Ernest Becker

Utopia is the form of ideal Society. Perhaps it is impossible to achieve it on Earth, but a wise man must place all his hopes in it.
- Plato, *The Republic*

Now after John was arrested, Jesus came to Galilee, proclaiming the good news of God, and saying, "The time is fulfilled, and the kingdom of God has come near; repent, and believe in the good news"
- Mark 1:14-15

(A). The Near Term

So what will life be like in a culture that offers its citizens methods for self-esteem/LIE construction under a Genuine Hero System? What types of activities will members of such a society be motivated to pursue?

This chapter will attempt to peer into the future and describe the world as it may look once the precepts of this Manifesto have been adopted and are being followed by the humans within their respective cultures or singly under a unified world government.

First, citizens in a Genuine Hero System culture will be raised from childhood to believe in the sanctity of all life, human and non-human; and, that the human species is a wondrous development after long eons in the evolution of life whose existence must be lovingly revered, appreciated and eternally sustained. They will rejoice in the mere fact of being human, and will revel in their creatureliness. And of course, they will rejoice in being a part of the natural and spiritual Cosmos, of being a part of the as-of-yet-uncomprehened God concept.

A function of such an attitude is that one's creatureliness will not be abhorred, as it is in cultures that fear and shrink from death, but embraced as a marvelous advance of nature. The human body will be admired and respected, not like it is now – hidden and scorned, or turned into an object of perversion and deviance.

The belief in the sanctity and importance of the species as a whole will also lend itself to instilling a respect and reverence for one's fellow man. Jesus' exaltation that one must love one's neighbor as yourself will be deemed more than mere aspiration, but akin to sacred law to be embraced and followed in one's everyday life. Indeed, such ideal will form the basis for one's attainment of self-esteem. Each individual life, including one's own, will be regarded with respect, admiration and wonder. Self-esteem will thus be measured not by one's material possessions or intellectual and spiritual assets or accomplishments, but what one gives in the collective human effort of improving the quality and quantity of life for others. Thus, obtaining a position in the education, medical fields, or in biological research, will be prized and monetarily and emotionally rewarded because those fields will be seen as offering an essential contribution to furthering the quality of life, as well as quantity of life, for everyone.

The belief in the sanctity of individual life of course compliments the sister belief underlying the Genuine Hero System that the human species is a special and sacred achievement of the evolution of life meriting eternal survival. Thus, self-worth will be derived from activities advancing that end. The most high regarded occupations will be in the sciences or technology fields, especially those that advance conservation and proper use of and interaction with the environment, the means to interdict natural cataclysms, and, of course, space exploration.

In short, the Genuine Hero System will inspire and reward service to one's fellow man and the human species through scientific, educational, or technological pursuits or occupations. High honor and celebrity will thus stem from one's superior achievements in those areas, rather than in the more trivial achievements from athletic prowess or other purely entertainment sources where one's "talent" is related to inherited physical attributes rather than on thoughtful and spiritual dedication to one's fellow man and species.

Religious practice and devotion also will be much changed in a Genuine Hero System culture. The ancient religions will have waned, so that no one attends church, the synagogue, masque or temple. While certain of the precepts of the old religions may be subsumed into the new religion of the genuine heroism, such precepts will likely be more useful in inspiring acts of love, consideration and service toward one's fellow man rather than in constructing a new theology or vision of God. Rather, spiritual discourses will be devised and offered that are based upon the latest scientific and philosophical discoveries, as well as spiritual and intellectual musings, in order to provide the individual with a current sense of the true nature of God and the Cosmos, rather than some dictated, inflexible dogma for the existence of a supreme entity.

This is not to say that a portion of one's self-esteem cannot be derived from methods offered by current hero systems, such as athletic endeavors, including spectator-ism, romantic love or lust, group politics, and other diversions which, standing on their own, are deemed to be trivial and counter to the advancement of the species to a higher level. There will always be a place for such other "trivial" methods of self-esteem creation and death denial in Genuine Hero System cultures since those pursuits are required to satisfy basic instinctual needs, such a procreation, inspire higher values or serve to help repress, however trivially, the reality of death.

The problem is not that these methods are pursued, but that other methods which advance humanity to its highest potential, such as through scientific examination and thought, are given only minimal importance in present cultures. Of course, methods of self-esteem construction which cause violent behavior or are otherwise inimical to achieving mankind's highest potential will not be offered by a Genuine Hero System culture. Thus, warfare and other forms of violence will be at long last be verboten as a means for settling internecine disputes within and without cultural groupings.

(B). <u>The Far, Far Term</u>

In *The Singularity Is Near*, Ray Kurzweil divides the advance of life into six stages or "epochs." In Epoch 3, animal brains emerge from the evolution of life and eventually evolve into the human mind. By Epoch 5, human intelligence has merged with technology and by Epoch 6, Kurzweil submits, "The Universe Wakes Up."

Under the Kurzweil formula, it may be the destiny of mankind, if Becker's dire prognosis can be averted by the implementation of the genuine hero system among and across human cultures, and then into a single, unified culture, to evolve in tandem with the technological advances made under such culture, to ultimately infuse the Universe Itself with awareness and understanding. When life, through the vehicle of the human species, has evolved to Epoch 6, Kurzweil believes: "Patterns of matter and energy in the universe become saturated with intelligent processes and knowledge" as "vastly expanded human intelligence (predominately non-biological) spreads through the universe."

Thus, Kurzweil's continuum of evolutionary destiny assigns the grave and profound obligation on humanity of achieving sentience for the Universe. This is very much akin to the quest for God which is posited as the central spiritual or religious belief of the Genuine Hero System. Thus, it is a belief based upon not only gaining comprehension of God through an epic quest, but giving God via His Cosmos, consciousness. This quest posits a starting point, at which we are presently located, wherein we have developed rather juvenile and simple-minded descriptions for God and the Cosmos, and explanations regarding God's relationship with the Cosmos and mankind, in the religious theologies that have arisen among past and present human cultures as exemplified by Christianity and Islam. Of course, more advanced and sophisticated theories regarding the existence and nature of God and the Cosmos have been proffered, especially in the last 250 years, based upon the latest scientific discoveries regarding the composition and structure of matter and space as expressed in the study of quantum mechanics and cosmological science.

The starting point for this quest for God must begin with the recognition that we don't know very much about the nature of God and the Cosmos because our understanding of those concepts has been stunted and slowed by dogmatic religious censure. Once that truism is accepted, once we acknowledge that we don't know God, we must dedicate our focus to a kind of passionate scientific, intellectual and spiritual study of God and the Cosmos. And the more advanced we become in doing so, the clearer the picture will become as to what God is, like a puzzle slowing coming together to form a whole image piece by tedious piece. After the passage of hundreds, and then thousands of years, we shall gain such a clear understanding of God as to permit the collective human mind to awaken and join with that superior intelligence as One eternal being.

Chapter Eighteen
Afterward: Doom or Salvation?

To recognize one's own insanity is, of course, the arising of sanity,
the beginning of healing and transcendence.
- Eckhart Tolle

We shall require a substantially new manner of thinking
if mankind is to survive.
- Albert Einstein

Ernest Becker feared that the evolutionary trait of intelligence and its offspring - awareness of one's creatureliness and inevitable death, fueled by the urge to self-preservation, may ironically doom the human species to extinction. As he put it in <u>Escape From Evil</u>:

The tragedy of evolution is that it created a limited animal with unlimited horizons. Man is the only animal that is not armed with the natural instinctive mechanism or programming for shrinking his world down to a size that he can automatically act on.

Intelligence gave the individual the horrible knowledge that he or she is an animal destined for eventual and inevitable decay and death. And worse, there was no way of knowing with any certainty what came after death. There is no way to prove, or disprove, no matter how good the writer, whether one's personality and soul lives on or ceases to exist after the physical body dies.

There is, of course, always the nagging fear that there is nothing but oblivion after the death of the body. If so, everything one accomplished (or failed to accomplish) during the course of one's life would be rendered meaningless and forgotten, for the most part, in the due course of time. To conceal this terrible truth, human beings, through the methods offered by the cultures in which they live, devise complicated symbolic illusions and rituals to hide or overcome the awful reality of death and for infusing their lives with meaning.

However, these symbolic mechanisms inspire the kind of trivial and destructive behavior which has stunted mankind's potential, causing misery, strife and ignorance for the majority of human beings that portends doom for the species. As Becker put it:

> It seems that the experiment of man may well prove to be an evolutionary dead end, an impossible animal – one who, individually, needs for healthy action the very conduct that, on a general level, is destructive to him.

In other words, the awareness of this awful predicament, propels humanity to both greatness and evil destructiveness or banal achievement in a ceaseless, often senseless and impossible striving to eclipse his inevitable, tragic fate . Therefore, the awareness of death will lead to the destruction of humanity either by its own hand or due to the fact that mankind will not progress to a sufficient technological level to fend off natural cataclysm.

The trick then is to find the means through culture to heroically overcome death by symbolic methods that do not lead to destructive or trivial behavior on the part of individual members of that culture but that advance the species to a higher level of achievement. Stated another way, culture must offer methods of heroism which compel mankind to reach its highest potential as a species instead of wasting the gift of advanced intelligence.

This Manifesto has proposed those methods, through the magic of the Genuine Hero System, that puts the survival of the human species, individual happiness and comfort, and the quest for the true nature of God and the Cosmos, as the primary motivating factors for the individual and for culture. Re-setting the goals of culture based upon the beliefs underlying the Genuine Hero System will have the effect of re-setting the paradigm by which humanity lives. It is thus the zealous aim of this book to inspire the construction of a new illusion, a grand illusion, as Becker called it, based upon the methods of action offered by the Genuine Hero System, that will enable the human species to reach its true potential, one that is based upon the reality of life and death though without collapsing upon itself under the weight of so much honesty and truth.

Thus, this Manifesto prescribes a basic and essential transformation of the way human civilization is organized and governed and of the very way people live and operate in the natural world. One only needs to look around at the world to realize what an abject and sorry mess humanity has made of the lives of ordinary and even extraordinary men. This mess is the result of the socialization process of cultures that program us all to adopt action methods in order to satisfy our psychological need to deny the reality of death based upon false or insufficient beliefs which have arisen in cultures for doing so. We have cheated ourselves of greatness and minimized the quality of our lives and the prospects for the survival of our children, our grandchildren, and their progeny, by failing to recognize that our terror of death is the motivating force behind all human action. Death is the only reality of life which we have far too long failed to recognize. And the cost is evident: A dysfunctional species heading toward almost certain extinction either by manmade or natural causes.

Modern global civilization is spiraling out of control. All around us, humans are killing each other in unprecedented numbers, in tribal wars, or in murderous conflicts fueled by the nationalism, materialism, greed, or crazed and irrational religious fanaticism. Indeed, we have dipped so far in the maelstrom of dysfunctional heroism that some individuals believe becoming a suicide bomber is a valid method of attaining self-esteem and personal immortality. The ultimate LIE of the modern world is the occupation of suicide bomber.

Many human beings, inspired by the thrill of accumulating wealth and material things as their method for overcoming the reality of death, engage in greedy, selfish actions at the expense of others and the natural health of the planet. So many in the modern age are bereft of a faith in the existence of God, or have grown so intellectually and spiritually cynical that they embrace the idea that God does not exist at all – that there is no meaning whatsoever behind the existence of the Cosmos except for its existence itself. The lack of meaning is thus the basis for belief and action. The result of this cacophony of mistaken or misshapen belief and methods for self-esteem creation is the periodic explosion of our financial markets, waste of our natural environment, endless internal and external wars, the spread of pornography, sexual abuse, the rise of cults, the general decline of morality and so many other ills that no wonder there is a feeling that mankind is on the road to destruction.

This Manifesto has sought to explain the reasons for mankind's failures and inability to utilize the evolutionary gift of intelligence to its greatest advantage. The mass of humanity wallows in abject poverty and ignorance, the species remains subject to doom, and we have come no closer to an understanding of the nature of God and the Cosmos than the first humans simply and solely because we have adopted inadequate methods for the creation of individual self-esteem to properly and sufficiently attack those basic problems. We have become fully aware of these problems in the modern age because of the advent of globalization through the significant, though under-realized, advances in industrial, communication, and travel technologies. Thus, unless mankind embarks upon a revolutionary plan for organizing the members of its divergent cultures into a uniform civilization under a Genuine Hero System that programs its citizens to construct life illusions based upon belief methods motivating actions which improve the quality of life for others, enhance the survivability of the species, and embark on a quest to understand the true nature of God and the Cosmos, the problems besetting humanity will continue unabated and the species will remain on the path to certain doom.

In conclusion, this Manifesto implores each of you to go now and ponder your beliefs and the methods used in your daily lives to construct your life immortality elusion in your personal mission to alleviate if not overcome entirely the fear of the stark reality of death in your life. Go now and recognize how your LIE directs your actions. Go now and acknowledge how your actions fail to benefit your fellow man, the salvation of the species, or an understanding of the true nature of God and the Cosmos. Go now and meditate upon existence, and the nature of God and the Cosmos, and accept the reality of God as a mysterious and wonderful force in the Cosmos. Go now and reject and discard the present illusion directing your actions as completely inadequate and unsatisfying in providing your life with genuine meaning and purpose. Go now and adopt the beliefs of the Genuine Hero System that are based upon the sanctity of the individual, the human species, and God, in offering methods of self-esteem creation and life illusion construction that are dedicated to improving the quality of life for others, enhancing the survivability of the human species, and seeking the true nature of God and the Cosmos.

And once you have done all that, go and become a disciple of the message and creed of this Manifesto, and spread its word to everyone who will listen.

Go now, and become a Son of Man.

The End

BIBLIOGRAPHY

Anderson, Benedict *Imagined Communities: Reflections on the Origins and Spread of Nationalism.* Verso, 2006.

Asimov, Isaac "Nightfall," *The Complete Stories of Isaac Asimov*, Collins, 1995.

Becker, Ernest *The Structure of Evil: An Essay on the Unification of the Science of Man.* The Free Press, 1968.

The Denial of Death. The Free Press, 1973.

Escape From Evil. The Free Press, 1975.

Beinhocker, Eric *The Origin of Wealth: Evolution, Complexity, and the Radical Remaking of Economics.* Harvard Business School Press, 2006.

Bryne, Rhonda *The Secret.* Atria Books, 2006.

Bryson, Bill *A Short History of Nearly Everything.* Broadway Books, 2004.

Caputo, Phil *A Rumor of War.* Holt Paperbacks, 1996.

Carveth, Donald "The Melancholic Existentialism of Ernest Becker," Free

Associations, Vol. 11, Part 3, No. 59 (2004), 422-27.

Clausewitz, Von Karl *On War.* Wilde Publications, 2008.

Collins, Francis S.   *The Language of God: A Scientist Presents Evidence for Belief.* Free Press, 2007.

Dawkins, Richard   *The Selfish Gene.* Oxford University Press USA, 2006

The God Delusion. Houghton Miffun Harcourt, 2006.

Darwin, Charles   *On the Origin of Species.* Dover Publications, 2006.

Dewey, Barbara   *As You Believe.* Bartholomew Books, 1985.

Dickens, Charles   "A Christmas Carol," *Stories For Christmas.* Platinum Press, 2000.

DiLorenzo, Thomas   *How Capitalism Saved America: The Untold Story of Our Country From the Pilgrims to the Present.* Three Rivers Press, 2005.

Fromm, Erich   *The Heart of Man: Its Genius for Good and Evil.* Harper and Row, 1964.

Gladwell, Malcolm   *The Tipping Point: How Little Things Can Make a Big Difference.* Little, Brown & Co., 2001.

Godin, Seth   *Unleashing the Ideavirus.* Hyperion, 2001.

Green, Celia   *The Human Evasion.* Institute of Psychophysical Research, 1977.

Hammett, Dashiel   *The Maltese Falcon.* Vintage, 1989.

Harris, Sam *The End of Faith: Religion, Terror and the Future of Reason.* W. W. Norton, 2005.

Hawking, Stephen *A Brief History of Time.* Bantam, 1998.

Helliwell, John *Globalization and Well-being.* University of British Columbia Press, 2003.

Hillman, James *A Terrible Love of War.* Penguin (Non-Classics), 2005.
Houellebecq, Michel *Atomized.* Vintage, 2001.

Judis, John B. "Death Grip," The New Republic (08/27/2007).

Karmis, Dimitrios *Theories of Federalism: A Reader.* Norman, Wayne Palgrave MacMillan, 2005.

Keegan, John *A History of Warfare.* Vintage, 1994.

Kurzweil, Ray *The Singularity is Near.* Penguin (Non-classics), 2006.

Liechty, Daniel *The Ernest Becker Reader.* The University of Washington Press, 2005.

The Matrix (Movie) Warner Home Video, 2007.

Monbiot, George *Manifesto For a New World Order.* New Press, 2006.

Osborne, Roger *Civilization: A New History of the Western World.* Penguin Books, 2008.

Rank, Otto   *Beyond Psychology.* Dover Books, 1958.

Rockwell, Llewellyn H. Jr.   "The Glory of War"
LewRockwell.Com (May 6, 2005)

Rossiter, Clinton ed.   *The Federalist Papers.* New
American Library, 1961.

Scheinfeld, Robert   *Busting Loose From the Money
Game.* John Wiley & Sons, Inc., 2006.

Smith, Adam   *The Wealth of Nations.* Bantam
Classics, 2003.

Solomon, Sheldon   "Tales From the Crypt: On the
Role of Death in Life,"

Greenberg, Jeff Pyszczynski, Tom Stark, Rodney
*Discovering God: The Origins of the Great Religions and
Evolution of Belief.* Harper One, 2008.

Thoreau, Henry David   *The Portable Thoreau.* Carl
Bode, ed. Penguin Books, 1964.

Tolstoy, Leo   *War and Peace.* Vintage Classics, 2008.

Yalom, Irving D.   *Staring at the Sun: Overcoming the
Terror of Death.* Jossey-Bass, 2008.

Zilboorg, Gregory   *Psychoanalysis and Religion.*
Farrar, Strauss & Cudahy, 1962.

A Message From the Author:

I first read Ernest Becker's *The Denial of Death* shortly after its publication in 1973 while in my sophomore year at the State University of New York at Binghamton. Needless to say, the book struck a chord that has stayed with me ever since. I simply knew that Becker's brilliant synthesis of psychological and sociological thought laid out in the book in developing his theory that death was the mainspring of human behavior was right on. Becker had found the key to human motivation – what makes humans do the things they do - and once the key was found, it seemed to me that opening the door to a culture that pursues human progress and survival was the logical next step.

In the 35 years since I first read *The Denial of Death*, and its successor, *Escape From Evil*, published posthumously in 1975, the kernel for the idea of a *Genuine Hero System* as the prescription for the establishment of the ideal human culture that could avoid Becker's dire prediction of doom for the species has been spawned, grown and evolved. Finally, after being diverted for long stretches by a legal career and raising a family, and writing speculative and crime fiction, in 2003, I set my mind to finally drafting **The Human Manifesto.**

Writing this Manifesto has become my life elusion – my method for gaining a kind of personal immortality by providing mankind with a self-help book to enable every human being to not only understand why they are driven to do the things they do, but also to prescribe for them, and society in general, the means to a truly benevolent, peaceful and advanced civilization that has a chance for

260

eternal salvation. It has also brought me closer to God – not the Catholic God of my upbringing and socialization as a member of the American cultural hero system, but the unknown God who has instilled within us a desire and drive to know Him.

This Manifesto is my small way of giving something to the human species, and in that way, to my children and their children. As Becker wrote as he closed *The Denial of Death*:

Who knows what form the forward momentum of life will take in the time ahead or what use it will make of our anguished searching. The most that any one of us can seem to do is to fashion something—an object or ourselves—and drop it into the confusion, make an offering of it, so to speak, to the life force.

This Manifesto is my offering.

Printed in the United States
151917LV00001B/12/P

9 781934 937808